MOLYNEUX

MOLYNEUX

The Interior Design of Juan Pablo Molyneux

Text by Michael Frank

RIZZOLI
NEW YORK

First published in the United States of America in 1997 by
Rizzoli International Publications, Inc.
300 Park Avenue South, New York, NY 10010

Photography Credits (referred to volume page numbers)

Jaime Ardiles Arce: 188, 191; Fernando Bengoechea: 103, 111; Scott Bowron: 98, 140 top, 140 bottom, 141 top, 141 bottom, 189; Billy Cunningham: 8, 13, 16, 17, 76, 78-79, 80, 82-83, 84, 85, 86-87, 87, 88, 89, 90-91, 92, 94, 94-95, 100-101, 102-103, 104-105, 106, 107 top, 107 bottom, 108, 109, 110, 134, 136, 137 top, 137 bottom, 138, 139, 142, 143, 158, 160, 161, 162, 163 top, 163 bottom, 164, 165, 166-167, 168, 169, 170, 171, 173 top, 173 bottom, 174, 175, 176-177, 178, 180-181, 181 top, 181 bottom, 182, 184 top, 184 bottom, 185, 186-187, 187; Jacques Dirand: 26, 28-29, 30, 31, 33; Carlos Eguiguren: 96-97, 197, 199; Alex McLean: 45, 48-49, 51; Jock Pottel: 201; Peter Vitale: 190, 194-195, 203, 204-205, 206, 207; Charles S. White: 144, 147, 148-149, 149, 151, 154 bottom, 156.

Photograph by Roberto Schezen, © Rizzoli International Publications, Inc.: 36.

Photograph by Billy Cunningham, © Tiffany & Co. Archives: 193.

Photographs by Billy Cunningham. Courtesy Architectural Digest, © 1991 The Conde Nast Publications. Used with permission: 54-55, 56-57, 58, 58-59, 61, 62, 63; © 1994 The Conde Nast Publications. Used with permission: 125, 126, 127, 128-129, 129, 130, 131, 132-133.

Photograph by Feliciano. Courtesy Architectural Digest, © 1995 The Conde Nast Publications. Used with permission: 208.

Photographs by Dan Forer. Courtesy Architectural Digest, © 1991 The Conde Nast Publications. Used with permission: 34, 37, 38-39, 40-41, 42, 43, 44, 46, 50; © 1992 The Conde Nast Publications. Used with permission: 18-19, 21, 23.

Photographs by Paulo Sabugosa. Courtesy Architectural Digest, © 1992 The Conde Nast Publications. Used with permission: 15, 64, 66, 68-69, 70-71, 72-73, 74, 75.

Photographs by Durston Saylor. Courtesy Architectural Digest, © 1989 The Conde Nast Publications. Used with permission: 2, 113, 114-115, 116-117, 118, 119, 120-121, 122, 123.

Photographs by Charles S. White. Courtesy Architectural Digest, © 1996 The Conde Nast Publications. Used with pemission: 146, 150, 152-153, 155, 157.

Library of Congress Cataloging-in-Publication Data

Frank, Michael (Michael R.), 1959–
    Molyneux : the interior design of Juan Pablo Molyneux / by Michael
Frank.
      p.   cm.
     ISBN 0-8478-2063-7
    1. Molyneux, Juan Pablo, 1946– —Criticism and interpretation.
    2. Decoration and ornament—United States—Neoclassicism.
    I. Molyneux, Juan Pablo, 1946– II. Title.
NK2004.3.M66F73 1997
747.2—dc21   97-18502
                       CIP

Designed by Marcus Ratliff, Inc., New York

COVER PHOTOGRAPH: The Palladian doghouse Molyneux designed for a charity benefit in 1992.

BACK COVER PHOTOGRAPH: Photograph by Billy Cunningham. Courtesy Architectural Digest, © 1996 The Conde Nast Publications. Used with permission.

TITLE PAGE: The entry hall at Goodwood, Molyneux's country house, with the Palladian doghouse in the foreground.

Printed and bound in Italy

CONTENTS

9   INTRODUCTION

27   CHAPTER ONE
A Park Avenue Penthouse

35   CHAPTER TWO
Molyneux Meets Mizner: Palm Beach

53   CHAPTER THREE
A Pied-à-Terre on Manhattan's Upper West Side

65   CHAPTER FOUR
The Invention of an Interior: Buenos Aires

77   CHAPTER FIVE
Remaking a Town House on Manhattan's Upper East Side

99   CHAPTER SIX
Molyneux at Home

135   CHAPTER SEVEN
Transforming an Apartment on Park Avenue

145   CHAPTER EIGHT
A Bicultural Journey in Laguna Beach

159   CHAPTER NINE
Vail Revisited

169   CHAPTER TEN
Trump Tower Aerie

179   CHAPTER ELEVEN
A Fifth Avenue Flat

189   CHAPTER TWELVE
Molyneux at Kips Bay and at Large

LIGHT MAHOGANY

WHITE BIRCH

LIGHT MAHOGANY

WHITE BIRCH W/ GREEN TINT

WHITE BIRCH

DESIGN TO BE REPEATED IN A SQUARES

LIGHT MAHOGANY

WHITE BIRCH

DARKER WHITE BIRCH

DARK MAHOGANY

WHITE BIRCH

DARK MAHOGANY

WHITE BIRCH

EBONY BORDER (INCLUDING OUTSIDE HALLWAY)

ACKNOWLEDGMENTS

I HAVE ALWAYS THOUGHT of my work as a magnificent opportunity to choose things from different sources and places and combine them to produce new and different takes on reality. Now, after some years in the design business, I've had a similar feeling, only with people instead of rooms.

Among the people who made it possible to put this book together were first, of course, my clients and my staff, without whom there would *be* no projects. Paige Rense, the editor in chief of *Architectural Digest*, has provided guidance and a sustaining belief in my work that have been vital at every turn. I would also like to thank Mrs. Allan MacDougall, Honorary Chairman of the Kips Bay Boys and Girls Club, whose combination of audacity and kindness I so admire, and Michael Frank, for his patience and his ability to assess my work and help to tell my stories.

I'm grateful, too, to the staff at Rizzoli, particularly Solveig Williams, Elizabeth White, and Barbara Einzig; the staff at *Architectural Digest*, notably James Huntington and Danita Wright; Lisa Lindblad, a source of wonderful support and coordinating skills; Marcus Ratliff, who possesses abundant understanding as well as a keen eye for book design; and the many photographers whose images appear in these pages. Their work has enhanced my work, and I am indebted to them all.

Finally, I would like to dedicate this book to my wife Pilar, who, surrounded by Matthew, Flossie, Urbano, and Nigel, really did it all.

—Juan Pablo Molyneux

The design for a painted marquetry floor Molyneux added to an apartment on East 64th Street.

*J*UAN PABLO MOLYNEUX was not born the full-fledged designer of the urbane, polished, and often neoclassical interiors for which he is best known. The architecturally confident rooms that fill these pages are the product of a lifetime of study, observation, and a good deal of trial and error. Like many journeys of creative development, Molyneux's has been accompanied by its share of fits and starts, but he has been careful to learn even from the early influences he later chose to react against. The versatility of Molyneux's present design vocabulary owes a good deal to his coming of age in the aesthetically strict world of modernism and then opening himself up to the more historically oriented realm of neoclassicism. It is in this combination that he has found his most suitable, his most comfortable, home.

Born in Santiago, Chile, in 1946, Molyneux comes from a family that is partly English by background. There is a hint of magical realism in his ancestry: his maternal grandfather, in the course of a worldwide grand tour, departed from London and tried to reach Australia by crossing the Andes on a mule; losing his way, he ended up on the doorstep of a farm in Chile, where he met, wooed, and married the beautiful young daughter of the house. Juan Pablo himself is very much a citizen of the world, the well-traveled son of well-traveled parents. He grew up speaking Spanish, French, and English and was a day student at The Grange, a boarding school in Santiago that was "like a little English colony—we had rugby, cricket, and detention on Saturdays." It is in part to this experience, and to his family, that Molyneux attributes his fondness for things English: paneled libraries, Regency furniture, and a patina of age and elegance that develops out of being rooted in one place for generations.

Molyneux's hybrid family background and his wide travels contribute palpably to the ease with which he now moves through different aesthetic styles and traditions, but this was not always the case. In 1964, Molyneux entered the architecture program at the Catholic University of Santiago, where students were trained under the rigorous discipline of Le Corbusian modernism, and the reigning figures were Mies van der Rohe and Walter Gropius. "We studied absolutely nothing classical at all. It was as

The marquetry floor designed by Molyneux for an apartment on East 64th Street, the realization of the sketch on the previous page.

if the history of architecture began with the twentieth century," Molyneux recalls. "We were pushed very much toward engineering, a socially conscious approach that was very typical of the period."

Molyneux remembers being thrilled with what he was learning at the time, yet there was a side of him that had always appreciated the old and the traditional, and he decided to spend the following academic year in Paris. He enrolled at the École des Beaux-Arts, where his first assignment was to design an orangerie for a chateau. "It was a failure," Molyneux remembers. "I had no training. I picked up the pencil and didn't know what to do." Gradually, he acquired a classical design and architecture vocabulary, and he began to assemble his own eclectic pantheon of influences: Jacques Ange Gabriel, architect of Le Petit Trianon at Versailles, which Molyneux considers one of the most "gracefully precise" buildings ever designed; the ancient Egyptians for "the monumentality and the contemporary spirit" of their structures; Andrea Palladio, understandably enough, "the great master to whom I return again and again for inspiration and guidance"; and, of course, the "long and noble reach" of Greco-Roman architecture.

Over the next six years, Molyneux divided his time between Santiago and Paris. It was a very conflicted period for the emerging designer. "In Santiago, the École des Beaux-Arts was considered very old-fashioned," he says. "I received no reassurance or confirmation of what I was learning in Paris. The attitude was, 'We don't do columns or rotundas here.' I think this is partly why—of course I only understand this now—I could not go on living in Chile. I felt temporary there, and somehow out of place." Even in Paris, Molyneux adds, the Beaux-Arts was not exactly the cutting edge: the late 1960s was a time of great social unrest in France, and the "establishment" was being aggressively challenged.

The two Santiago homes Molyneux's family lived in during this period offer clues to his early conflict. First, there was the house he grew up in, a French, neo-classical, brick and stucco structure that, while not particularly distinguished architecturally, nonetheless had a formative influence. The interiors, which his mother did herself, were mostly traditional, with antique French and English furniture that had been passed down through his family, good rugs, and seventeenth- and eighteenth-century tapestries, for which Molyneux has retained a strong affection (they continue to turn up in many of his more formal and even some of his informal projects).

Then, in the late sixties, his family decided to move into a contemporary apartment. Molyneux's own quarters were his first stab at interior design, and, casual though they were, they did favor the modernist over the neoclassical: he used French

Molyneux's first apartment in Santiago, which he designed in the early 1970s.

UPPER LEFT: His bedroom, featuring a French Empire daybed.

OTHER VIEWS: The living room, shown in two different incarnations, with whitewashed walls and (during a later period) with walls and ceiling in black lacquer. The mixture of elements, characteristic of Molyneux's work at the time, includes a contemporary coffee table, which he designed, and a Louis XVI armchair.

blue sisal wall-to-wall carpeting, white plastered walls textured with a coarse brush, curtains made of unlined burlap, a Calder mobile, and a German poster for the film *The Seven Samurai*, which he glued to the ceiling. "The apartment was on the eighth floor of the building, and I spent many hours on the street looking up at that effect, thinking I was an absolute genius!" Molyneux says dryly. "Let's say that it was a phase that passed—rather soon, fortunately."

After he finished his schooling, Molyneux traveled throughout North and South America, Africa, Russia, and again and again to Europe. He went into business in Santiago in the early 1970s and, as one of his earliest commissions, designed a large studio for an international fashion model. Molyneux addressed his client's need to accommodate many guests by creating a kind of amphitheater in the space, a progression of receding platforms that reached all the way to the back wall. On some he set mattresses; on others, pillows; on still others, decorative objects. In this innovative solution, Molyneux for the first time applied his classical training to a design challenge. In a vivid foreshadowing of his mature work, his choice of an amphitheater was strongly architectural, an obvious Greco-Roman allusion, while the actual finishes in the apartment remained largely contemporary.

Also in the early seventies, Molyneux set up his own interior design business, construction company, and retail shop in Santiago, where he sold antiques, decorative objects, and furniture he designed. The Chilean phase of his career culminated in 1975, with an exhibition of his work at the Museo de Bellas Artes. It was two years after the coup, a bleak period, and Molyneux welcomed the opportunity to assemble an array of furniture, carpets, china, ceramics, and fabrics, all of his own design and many created specifically for the show. The exhibition ran for three weeks, and when it closed, Molyneux felt depleted and adrift. There was not a great deal of design work in Chile, and he sensed he had reached a critical moment in his career.

By 1975, the year Juan Pablo and his wife, Pilar, were married, he had relocated both his business and his home to Buenos Aires, a city he found more cosmopolitan and stimulating. Over the next decade, his business grew substantially. "Buenos Aires is very neoclassical, heavily influenced by nineteenth-century French architecture," says Molyneux. "As my work was becoming more neoclassical, more like it is now, it meshed well with both the city's buildings and its sensibility." Molyneux thrived in Buenos Aires for ten years, but gradually he recognized that his restlessness was returning. "I started out in Santiago, with a rather modest canvas," he explains. "In Buenos Aires, my canvas became broader and richer. But something was missing. I felt I was becoming complacent. I wanted more of a challenge."

Creative people in many fields who are seeking a challenge are often drawn to New York, and Molyneux was no exception. He had visited the city on shopping trips with clients and was impressed with the way New York was organized for his field, with its wide range of design sources and antique dealers, its varied and vibrant architecture, its great energy and verve, and, he confesses readily, the quality of the competition. In the mid-eighties, Molyneux dipped his toe into the New York waters: he met a prospective client, who had seen his work in South America. He took this first job in New York, then a second, then a third, traveling back and forth for a number of years between Argentina and the States. Eventually he decided to make a complete break, and by 1987 he was living and working in New York full-time.

Russian-style painted marquetry floor designed by Molyneux for an apartment on Park Avenue near East 64th Street. The jardiniere is nineteenth-century Russian.

*T*he design work collected in this book, the work of Juan Pablo Molyneux's maturity, dates from the period when he first established himself in New York, in 1985 or so, and continues up to the present. The projects tend to fall into two groups: houses or apartments that Molyneux has restored and reinvented, and those that he has created more or less from scratch. In both cases, Molyneux insists on studying, mulling over, and responding to the existing architecture. His respect, however, is never doctrinaire. Old, he believes, is never worth preserving simply because it is old. Architects, builders, and designers made mistakes in the past, just as they make mistakes in the present. Molyneux's goal, always, is to enter into a dialogue with a space and figure out how he can bring out its best side, or supply a best side if it is lacking. He is seldom interested in strict or literal historical preservation; his interiors have been made in the present, and he wants this to be apparent. Despite his neoclassical vocabulary, there is still a good deal of the contemporary in his work: his floor plans are efficient and practical; his upholstered furniture is comfortable and durable; he is interested in new technologies (poured rather than carved stone, for example) that help him bury the functional (pipes, electrical wires) in the aesthetic (a classical fireplace); he likes to combine antique furniture with contemporary pieces of his own design.

Molyneux is seldom rigid, although certain ideas, approaches, and principles recur again and again in his work. He believes that every house or apartment, no matter how informal, should have a clearly defined entryway. He has created grand ones (the rotunda in Buenos Aires seen here, the gallery on Park Avenue [p. 134]) and more modest versions. Similarly, interiors, especially large ones, require what Molyneux calls a "center of distribution": a space, a hall or gallery, that directs the flow of traffic through the interior, while at the same time serving as an introduction to, and setting the tone for, the rest of the home. Sometimes the center of distribution is the same room as the entryway (Park Avenue [p. 134]); sometimes it is separate, as in Molyneux's own house in Vail seen in Chapter Six, or in the case of the Upper East Side town house (p. 78). Always, it receives some of the designer's most disciplined thinking.

Molyneux insists upon paying close attention to setting. "What's going on beyond your windows is important," he maintains. "You either harmonize with it or position yourself in contrast to it, but you must consider it, no matter what." Fabrics, colors, patterns, materials, finishes, and furniture suitable to the town house on

The neoclassical rotunda from Buenos Aires (see Chapter Four).

Manhattan's Upper East Side featured in Chapter Five, for instance, are entirely
different from those in Palm Beach (Chapter Two) or Vail (Chapter Nine). This does
not mean that a house at the beach is upholstered in blue and white cotton or a
house in the Berkshires is decked out in rag rugs and patchwork quilts. Molyneux's
approach is much subtler and more nuanced. In both formal and informal interiors
alike, he often creates connections between objects and across periods. Molyneux's
ease with different countries and centuries reflects his diverse background and edu-
cation, as well as common sense: rooms fitted out with objects from only one period
tend to be stiff and monotonous, no matter how good the furniture.

Molyneux is, of course, adept in his use of columns, pilasters, pediments,
architraves, wainscoting, and strongly proportioned moldings. This is, after all, what
makes his interiors neoclassical. Yet at the same time he is extremely fond of trompe
l'oeil: the illusion of architecture, marble, marquetry, scenery, or "serious" paintings
often appeals to him as much as the real thing, especially when the two are combined.
He is particularly interested in the relationship between the limitations of architecture

A solarium in Lyford Cay, with
trompe l'oeil in progress (above)
and completed (right). The
tropical-motif rug was made
in Portugal.

The entry hall in Lyford Cay. The carved baseboard, columns, and moldings are made of local coquina stone. The nineteenth-century table is Indo-Portuguese and is inlaid with bone.

and the freedom of trompe l'oeil. Molyneux is not finicky about how he introduces classical detailing; indeed, there is something about the wit and lightheartedness of trompe l'oeil that he often prefers to the real thing. "With trompe l'oeil," the designer observes, "you can create spaces, moods, shapes. It's not fake. That's what people usually say, and it's wrong. Trompe l'oeil is a fantasy that *provokes* reality."

Molyneux turns to trompe l'oeil when faced with a variety of architectural challenges. In a plain room, he uses it to provide architecture, as for example the Pompeiian gallery he installed in an apartment on Park Avenue near 64th Street, whose elaborate wainscoting, columns, arches, and glimpses of garden are all invented. In so theatrically detailed a space, Molyneux believes, you dispense with the need for furniture entirely; the room stands on its own.

In an interior without views, trompe l'oeil can create them, as in the dining room of the Park Avenue penthouse featured in the first chapter (see p. 30) or in the living room Molyneux designed for a house in the Bahamas, to which he added an imagined seascape across from the actual one (p. 23). In Palm Beach, Molyneux used trompe l'oeil to opposite effect. In Addison Mizner's cavernous living room, which is more than forty feet in length, the designer added a balustrade and storm-tossed sky to the ceiling, which, he argues, paradoxically helps *contain* the room. "If I'd decorated it with moldings, it would have been very heavy. You have to take into account the volume of a room when you decide how to treat its surfaces."

For the stairwell at Palm Beach, Molyneux commissioned one of the pieces of trompe l'oeil of which he is most proud, an atelier of "old master" paintings and sculpture. The atelier alludes to his client's art collection, but as with most of Molyneux's trompe l'oeil, it serves a design purpose as well. Here too, Molyneux was confronted with a problematic space: a large library that was open, on its fourth wall, to the dramatic stairwell. Without the trompe l'oeil, the staircase was too grand and bore little relationship to the room. The trompe l'oeil managed to domesticate the staircase, address a theme in the client's life, and remain playful at the same time.

Molyneux's playfulness continues in his treatment of floors, which he thinks of as the sixth facade or elevation, following the four walls and the ceiling. He considers them especially important in American domestic architecture, where, unlike in Europe, ceilings tend to be low and plain. The designer takes three basic approaches to his floors. He creates a relationship between them and the walls, either by integrating these surfaces or playing them off one another; he uses the floor to reflect a ceiling; and he uses the floor to replace a ceiling—not literally, of course, but in terms of the architectural interest it introduces into an interior.

The living room in Lyford Cay,
with Lucretia Moroni's trompe
l'oeil mural, reinterpreting the
seascape that is seen through the
primary windows. The needlepoint rug, a Molyneux design,
features coral motifs.

A preparatory drawing for a rug
Molyneux designed for a dining
room/library in Hobe Sound,
Florida.

The Pompeiian gallery on Park Avenue is an example of one of Molyneux's integrative designs. The faux mosaic floor here continues the trompe l'oeil architectural fantasy of columns, arches, and trelliswork on the walls. Elsewhere in the same apartment, Molyneux used Russian-inflected painted marquetry floors. The designer's goal is not to integrate these floors with his concept of the walls so much as to play off of them. His faux marquetry, which turns up again in his 1995 Kips Bay living room and elsewhere, is exceedingly architectural and very much stands on its own, almost as a painting or a piece of furniture might. Indeed, Molyneux concedes that these floors probably have their strongest connection to the Regency or eighteenth-century furniture with which they are often paired.

The marble floors in Molyneux's strongly neoclassical galleries—prime examples are Buenos Aires and Park Avenue (pp. 64 and 134, respectively)—are often carefully calibrated to reflect the beam work in the ceilings, even if this beam work is, in turn, a creation of the drafting table. These floors, like the walls and ceilings that envelop them, are tightly, almost mathematically, conceived in their use of precise geometric motifs. Molyneux is looser and more whimsical in the floors he uses to "replace" a ceiling; among these are the carpet he created for the library of the Upper East Side town house, whose motifs are drawn from eighteenth-century ceiling moldings, and the rug he used in the dining room-library at Hobe Sound, whose birds, flowers, and monkeys allude to the tropical setting.

Juan Pablo Molyneux's work is very much about building intricate relationships—between floors and ceilings, walls and floors, rooms that adjoin one another, rooms that open onto terraces, terraces that lead into gardens. And, of course, he builds a relationship between a client and his habitat. Many consultations and conversations take place before Molyneux sits down to the drafting table or visits a showroom or antique dealer. Molyneux is probing, observant, and curious about people, and he is always careful to take his cues from how his clients live, dress, and travel, the paintings and furniture they collect, and the way they intend to use the house or apartment.

Juan Pablo loves design—this is evident in the gusto with which he talks about it. He doesn't mind mocking himself, and this levity comes through in both what he creates and the way he reflects upon it. He takes pride in his work. He insists on the highest level of craftsmanship possible; nothing in his rooms is makeshift or make-do. In New York, the city of constant movement, Molyneux tries to bring a sense of permanence and rootedness to what he does. In New York and elsewhere, his interiors are built to last.

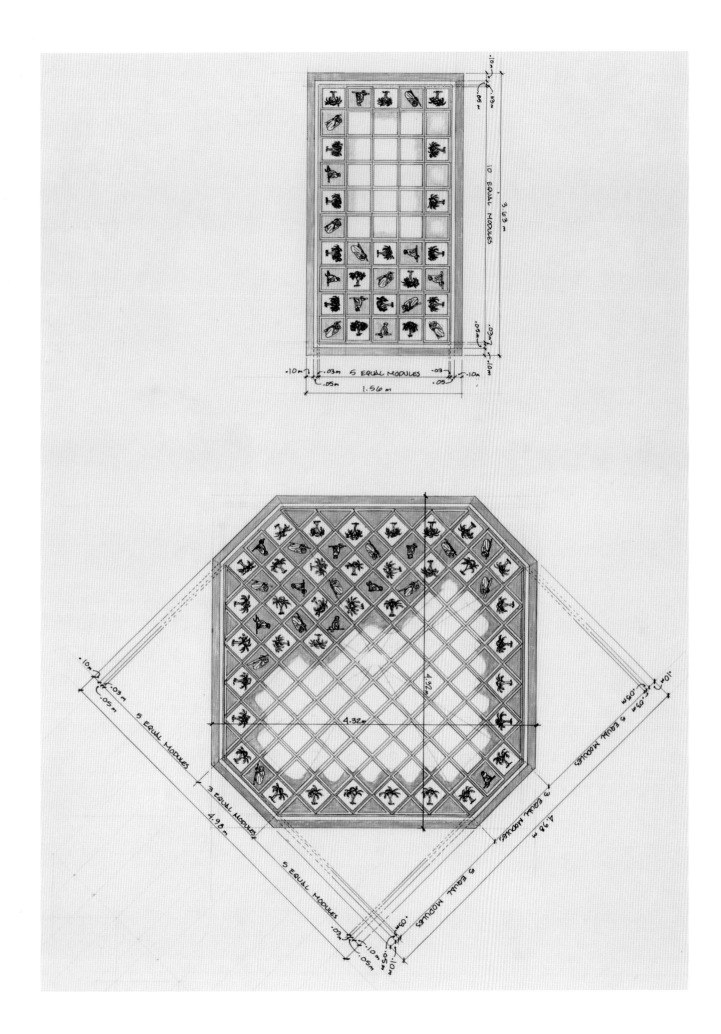

10 EQUAL MODULES

3.03 m

.10m

.05 m

.10m

.03m 5 EQUAL MODULES .03

.05m

1.56 m

.10m

.03 m

.05 m

5 EQUAL MODULES

3 EQUAL MODULES

4.98 m

5 EQUAL MODULES

4.32m

4.32 m

.10m

.05 m

5 EQUAL MODULES

3 EQUAL MODULES

4.98 m

5 EQUAL MODULES

.10m

.05m

.03m

CHAPTER ONE

A Park Avenue Penthouse

A MONG THE FIRST INTERIORS Molyneux completed during the mid-eighties, when he was continuing to work in both Buenos Aires and New York, this Park Avenue penthouse represents an interesting transitional project. It is transitional in more than one sense: first because it still reflects the more contemporary flavor of Molyneux's work in Santiago and Buenos Aires (some of the furniture, indeed, was exhibited in his show at the Museo de Bellas Artes in 1975); but also because Molyneux's work here is less architectural—less structural—than it was to become over the next decade.

This was partly a function of his clients' requests and partly a result of the condition of the apartment when Molyneux came on the scene. Designed in 1929 by the gifted architect Rosario Candela, the building represented, according to architectural historian Elizabeth Hawes, "all that Park Avenue stood for on the eve of the Depression—solidity, security, and the height of luxury." [Elizabeth Hawes, *New York, New York: How the Apartment House Transformed the Life of the City*, 1993.] The interiors retained these qualities, although they had been stripped of all of Candela's classical detailing, including moldings, floors, and mantelpieces, during the previous owners' renovations. Molyneux's clients, in addition, embodied a duality similar to the one that characterized the first part of the designer's career: the husband's taste was contemporary, the wife's more classical. Molyneux's task was to find a compromise between the two, while at the same time managing to bring the apartment's large white spaces to life.

The whiteness derived from the earlier renovation, probably done in the mid-1970s, in which the original parquet was replaced with travertine, and the new Sheetrock walls were all painted the same cream color. There was no embellishment of any kind, and, typical of Park Avenue, the views were unimpressive. "Because my clients didn't want to do any architectural work," says Molyneux, "I could change the interiors only with portable elements and finishes. I saw my task as one of humanizing the space."

The entry hall, with the staircase that Molyneux likens to a "piece of sculpture."

FOLLOWING PAGES: The living room, where the tapestry is an eighteenth-century Belgian *feuille de choux*, the rugs are eighteenth-century Turkish, and the coffee table is one of Molyneux's designs from his Chilean period. "I think of this apartment, basically, as contemporary with antique notes," says the designer.

The dining room's trompe l'oeil views and ceiling by Lucretia Moroni open up the almost windowless space. Molyneux inserted authentic columns among the painted ones for an unexpected—and playful—touch of verisimilitude.

According to Hawes, Rosario Candela "invested unusual energy in the entry hall . . . because he thought it was important to greet a visitor with a full sense of home." Entryways are, of course, equally important to Molyneux, and his goal here was to create as dramatic an effect as possible. He began by removing a clumsy handrail on the staircase, which was otherwise one of the best additions made during the 1970s. This enhanced its sculptural quality and enabled Molyneux to undercut its modernist line by juxtaposing it against a Louis XV armchair and a Victorian chinoiserie chest arranged with Chinese porcelain. Molyneux introduced further traditional notes into the entry hall with an eighteenth-century Chinese Coromandel screen and an English Regency side table.

Another view of the entry hall, a space the building's architect, Rosario Candela, considered particularly important. "In a typical apartment," writes architectural historian Elizabeth Hawes, "...he made it a full-sized room with rich views into the interior, because he thought it was important to greet a visitor with a full sense of home." The screen to the right is eighteenth-century Coromandel with an aubergine background. The ostrich egg and silver candlesticks are Victorian.

He lacquered the entry hall and the living room in a color he calls *thé au lait*. A pale, milky brown, the walls, he says, "gained a sheen that helped enliven the surfaces. When there are no moldings, and your floors are basically white, it helps to play with the light in a room, which the lacquer does absolutely."

In the living room he took the edge off the cold travertine floors by covering them with two Chinese silk rugs. But his most dramatic—and characteristic—choice was the sixteenth-century Belgian *feuille de choux*, or cabbage leaf, tapestry whose rich colors and vivid curling cabbage leaves animate the room in an emphatic way. Molyneux found the tapestry in Buenos Aires and confesses that his clients were a little tepid about it until he hung it up. "Then they understood what I meant—even the husband, who resisted traditional things. It changed the space and created an opening through which I could bring in some period furniture." Among the antique pieces Molyneux chose for the room were a Queen Anne secretary and two tables from the eighteenth century, one English, the other Irish. He contrasted the warm burnished quality of the wood with several tables of his own design, one in glass and lapis and a matching pair in jasper and steel. "The furniture is very mixed," Molyneux says, "but the pieces have in common a certain scale and, I like to think, a certain quality too."

Molyneux decked out the dining room in trompe l'oeil by Lucretia Moroni, an artist whose imaginative work he went on to use in a number of ways in future projects. Here, he was solving a particular problem: the large, rather dark dining room had only one window. Molyneux installed four one-quarter columns, one in each corner, in order to supply a note of reality. He then quickly moved on to fantasy: a portico of columns and a balustrade that opens onto a Southern Italian aquatic landscape, and takes the place of the missing windows and views. On the ceiling, in a recessed circle that appears to be one of the few remaining Candela legacies, Molyneux asked Moroni to paint a cupola. "The room went from being a claustrophobic box to a kind of summer idyll," the designer says. "It was probably the most drastically transformed space in the apartment."

Molyneux has a good idea of when to transform and when to mask: the apartment, which had been owned previously by a movie producer, came with a fully furnished screening room that the new owners decided to leave for the moment. Molyneux made the "unspeakably ugly" chrome club chairs disappear by covering them with a collection of American patchwork quilts. "Sometimes you have to rethink a room entirely, but sometimes," he says, "you have to know when a simple gesture will do."

CHAPTER TWO

Molyneux Meets Mizner: Palm Beach

"I WAS APPALLED WHEN I FIRST SAW THIS HOUSE," Molyneux says of El Sarmiento, the 1923 Palm Beach mansion designed by Addison Mizner. It had recently been acquired by a long-time Molyneux client, who told him nothing about the house; he merely handed over a key and asked Juan Pablo to go take a look. Molyneux flew down to Florida. He knew Mizner's houses only from their facades; he'd never been inside one before. He found the spaces large, gloomy, and in considerable disrepair. Unfurnished, the living room reminded him of a cavernous hotel lobby from the 1940s. "The mixed-up style of the architecture confused me," Molyneux recalls, "the way the windows, for example, suddenly and for no apparent reason changed from one volume and period into another. The former owner had made all kinds of 'improvements': partitions, plastic tile in the bathrooms, lowered ceilings. To be honest, I didn't much care for what I found."

Molyneux felt that either he or the house was out of sync. He knew that he had to spend some time with Mizner, whose blending of different styles and periods he found perplexing. He decided to indulge a long-held fantasy of roller-skating through an empty building. "When you are going at a certain speed inside huge rooms, not a walking or a running speed, you start to feel every inch of every dimension in your body. I'm not suggesting that all architects or designers start skating on the job, but for me it was a way of breaking down the 'Mizner monster.'" After several hours, Molyneux began to understand the architect's appeal. Mixed up though the house was, somehow the total began to make sense. "The spaces are worked very beautifully," Molyneux says. "Mizner's architecture is without fear. Its boldness casts a spell on you."

Addison Mizner (1872–1933) was responsible for infusing 1920s Palm Beach with its elegant, though largely contrived, "Spanish" flavor, which might more accurately be called "Mediterranean hybrid." Beginning with the Everglades Club, which he designed in 1918 for sewing machine heir Paris Singer, Mizner eventually masterminded several dozen Palm Beach (and Boca Raton) houses, shops, and office and

The stairwell, featuring trompe l'oeil by Robert Archer and Emma Temple. Its subject is the Spanish School—but as it might be found in an eccentric artist's (or collector's) atelier.

LEFT: Exterior view of El Sarmiento, which Addison Mizner designed for Anthony J. Drexel Biddle in 1923.

RIGHT: A detail of the living room, where Francis Bacon's *Figure Turning* hangs over an eighteenth-century Italian commode that is modeled on a sarcophagus. The marble tabletop in the foreground is seventeenth-century Florentine intarsia.

apartment buildings that helped transform the town into the fashionable watering hole it became during the early decades of this century. He built his own factories and plants, where he produced the furniture, roof tiles, ironwork, lighting fixtures, and cast stone for moldings, columns, and balustrades that typified the Mizner look. Alva Johnston, Mizner's early, and rather critical, biographer, famously called his work, "Bastard-Spanish-Moorish-Romanesque-Gothic-Renaissance-Bull-Market-Damn-the-Expense Style" [Alva Johnston, *The Legendary Mizners*, 1953, cited in Donald W. Curl, *Mizner's Florida: American Resort Architecture*, 1992]. This may be hard, but it's not untrue. As Mizner himself once said,

> Most modern architects have spent their lives carrying out a period to the last letter and producing a characterless copybook effect. My ambition has been . . . to make a building look traditional and as though it had fought its way from a small unimportant structure to a great rambling house that took centuries of different needs and ups and downs of wealth to accomplish. I sometimes start a house with a Romanesque corner, pretend that it has fallen into disrepair and been added to in the Gothic spirit, when suddenly the great wealth of the New World has poured in and the owner had added a very rich Renaissance addition.
>
> [From Ida M. Tarbell, "Appreciation of a Layman," in *Florida Architecture of Addison Mizner*, 1928; reissued by Dover in 1992 with a new introduction by Donald W. Curl]

Lucretia Moroni's trompe l'oeil panels introduce a Gothic arch into the courtyard, where Doric columns and eclectic windows typify the mixture of styles that characterizes Mizner's architecture.

The loggia, with a view into the living room. Molyneux chose to furnish this space casually, with a combination of upholstered furniture and iron furniture by Diego Giacometti. Paintings, left to right, are by Picasso, Joan Mitchell, and Botero. The sculpture is by Alberto Giacometti. The wooden ceiling is original to the house.

LEFT: The sitting area in the guest room, with its original Mizner fireplace. The painting is by Soutine, the art deco sconces by Brandt, and the coffee table by Mies van der Rohe.

RIGHT: The guest room is reached by this lively hall, where once again Mizner's mixture of styles are evident in the classical columns, the Georgian-style over-door, and the Italianate rustic wooden ceiling. The painting over the table is by Tamayo; the sculpture in the foreground is Henry Moore's *Seated Armless Figure*.

Certainly this is true of El Sarmiento, which, in addition to its imaginary additions, received many actual ones over the years, beginning as early as 1927, when it underwent a substantial remodeling by Joseph Urban.

Molyneux's challenge was to restore El Sarmiento without feeding the "Mizner monster," while at the same time finding a way to express his own idea of the "different needs" and "ups and downs of wealth"—and fashion—that inform these grand interiors. Then too, there were architectural mistakes in the house; some Mizner's, others made during later renovations. Molyneux wasn't afraid to make changes: his idea of restoration has always been to revive the spirit and meaning of a place, not the actual historical artifact. In addition, of course, he had to take into

account the client's request for comfort and ease—the house is used four months a year by a large family who entertain frequently—and his own insistence on taking a cue, for his interiors, from the location. "Ideally a house near the water is made of a roof and columns and little else," Molyneux says. "That's impossible here, naturally, but I wanted that sense, that freshness and lightness."

Molyneux began by removing all of the previous owner's additions. This was easy enough, as he'd already erased them mentally during his roller-skating tour. Along the way, he discovered treasures, such as a painting of Neptune on the entry hall ceiling, which he took delight in restoring. But there were problems too. The library, for example, felt like an afterthought: it was open to the living room, a dreary

ABOVE: A detail of the entry hall. Molyneux added the marble trim and art-deco radiator cover to the fireplace. The radiator cover and sconces are both by Brandt. The painting is by Lucio Fontana; the chairs are by Diego Giacometti.

LEFT: The library "used to feel left over, the worst room in the house," says the designer, who brought a cosmopolitan mixture to the interior, where an eighteenth-century Boulle *bureau plat* meets a nineteenth-century Chinese rug, Tiffany lamps, and a table sculpture by Marino Marini.

patio, and the house's central stairwell. Molyneux closed the first two openings and added a wooden ceiling, with its beams and corbels. "I think it's the kind of change Mizner would have made if he'd had my job," says Molyneux. Some rooms he merely reassigned, such as the dining room, which now occupies the space originally used as a ballroom and is furnished with both dining and seating areas. The bathrooms were largely designed anew.

Molyneux knew all along that the house would be filled with the client's striking collection of modern paintings, among them works by Pablo Picasso, Francis Bacon, and Chaim Soutine, but he refused to look at the actual canvases until he had settled on his plans for the interiors. "I didn't want to prepare a gallery for the collection," Molyneux says. "And besides, the client is always moving them around." He does admit, though, to knowing about one painting, a Helen Frankenthaler, which because of its size (nearly twenty feet in length alone) was destined for the dining room, where there was a wall capacious enough to accommodate it properly.

Molyneux's affection for trompe l'oeil is evident throughout the house and in several rooms serves as a foundation for the interiors. In the entry hall, for example, he commissioned Lucretia Moroni to produce a faux Caucasian carpet on the slate floor; its tones are drawn from the room's ceiling, with its blue painting of Neptune set into an elaborate burnished wooden surround. In the living room, Moroni created an audacious architectural vista, complete with a crumbling, decayed balustrade (after Mizner's original on the house's exterior) and a cloud-tumbled blue sky. "The room was so safe," Molyneux says. "I told Lucretia I wanted something tempestuous." Indeed, it looks as if a fierce Florida—or maybe Neptune-commanded—storm has just lifted the ceiling off the serenely elegant room.

In the stairwell, Molyneux commissioned an ambitious trompe l'oeil from Robert Archer and Emma Temple. It depicts an atelier with a rather topsy-turvy and tongue-in-cheek collection of busts, tapestries, stretchers, and fragments of paintings from the Spanish School, complete with a piece of Velázquez's *Las Meninas* and Molyneux's own face peeking out from among the Goyas. The designer admits to having taken a risk: he didn't tell his serious art-collecting client about the irreverent decoration of the stairwell beforehand, but fortunately the gamble paid off. "When he saw it," Molyneux recalls, "he told me he preferred it to his own collection!"

In furnishing the interiors, Molyneux continued to interweave these three robust personalities, Mizner's, his client's, and his own. The client wanted the living room to have the feeling of a plush reading room, for instance, and insisted on comfortable upholstered furniture; Molyneux combined these contemporary pieces with

A detail of the dining room, which was once the house's ballroom. Molyneux designed the cabinet to display the owner's collection of pre-Columbian antiquities.

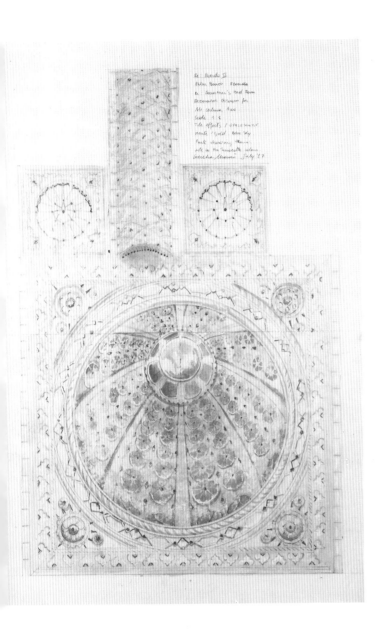

The daughter's bedroom has an elaborate trompe l'oeil ceiling by Lucretia Moroni. The cupola (preparatory sketch above) is deliberately off-center in order to show the best perspective to the occupant of the bed. Painting by Milton Avery.

four eighteenth-century French armchairs, a pair of seventeenth-century Florentine tables, and imposing canvases by Picasso, Bacon, Kees van Dongen, and Joan Mitchell. "The contrast," he says, "gives the room elegance, texture, and drama." In the dining room, Molyneux joined draped damask tables with an oversized California-style seating area and the owner's collection of pre-Columbian artifacts. In the library, Molyneux merged even more disparate elements: the desk is an eighteenth-century French *bureau plat*, the side table is seventeenth-century Spanish and exceedingly plain, the lamps are Tiffany, and none of the textiles belong together by any conventional measure. "The furnishings are like the paintings," Molyneux explains. "They don't match. They're independent. They're like Mizner."

Somehow—when it comes to independence, at any rate—they feel like they're Molyneux too.

LEFT: In order to create a more balanced space, Molyneux closed one of the living room's arches. Picasso's *Homme Assis au Verre* hangs over the former opening.

ABOVE: Overview of the living room, with a striking ceiling by Lucretia Moroni. Mizner was responsible for installing the eighteenth-century mantelpiece. The chairs in the foreground are Louis XVI, the rug a Molyneux design. From left to right are paintings by Picasso, Joan Mitchell, Lee Krasner, and Francis Bacon.

CHAPTER THREE

A Pied-à-Terre on Manhattan's Upper West Side

A RATHER DIFFERENT, more relaxed and playful side to Molyneux shines through in this next project, a New York pied-à-terre he designed for the children of the owners of El Sarmiento. The apartment is located in a 1909 neo-Gothic building by Harde & Short on the Upper West Side that was originally designed as artists' studios. This explains the beautiful proportions, the pure, milky, northern light, and the fact that from the entry hall you look down into the tall living room. In addition, the apartment has a close-up view of the Museum of Natural History and several pleasing, quintessentially Molyneux details, such as the Corinthian pilasters and elegant iron balustrade, which were already in place when Molyneux came on the scene. Although they probably weren't original to the apartment, the designer was delighted to find and incorporate them into his plan for the interiors.

His mission here was naturally much more informal than El Sarmiento. "The children asked for something young and lighthearted and European," the designer recalls. He knew that his clients were going to use the apartment at different times, so there was no need to change the floor plan and carve it up into bedrooms of equal sizes. (The apartment actually has three bedrooms, though one, a former maid's room, is quite small.) There was, in fact, less restructuring in this project than redesignating. Architecturally, the living room is exactly as Molyneux found it. The library occupies the space that was formerly used as a dining room, although he added the beams and the cherry paneling. Only the kitchen underwent a significant transformation. The space that was once three separate, awkward rooms (kitchen, breakfast room, and pantry) is now the apartment's combined kitchen and dining area. Molyneux readily points out that this space retains traces of its previous divisions. "The soffit, which contains the air conditioning, I left, as it was too complicated to move, and the windows are original. When renovating existing architecture, you can't always start over with a clean, perfect space. Sometimes this lends a good deal of character, even more than you anticipate."

In the new kitchen, Molyneux copied the paneling from the old breakfast

A detail of the faux mosaic floor by Lucretia Moroni.

53

Viewed here from the entry hall, the living room reveals its atelier-like proportions. Among its classical motifs are the Corinthian pilasters, the Greek key pattern on both the sisal rug and the iron table, and the ancient Roman torsos. The painting over the sofa is by Rauschenberg.

Another view of the living room. Symmetrical furniture arrangements center on wrought iron coffee tables. The fabric on the chairs is Fortuny; the painting is Andy Warhol's *Double Elvis*.

ABOVE: A detail of the entry hall, with a Biedermeyer piano said to have belonged to Elton John.

RIGHT: Formerly the apartment's dining room, the library received considerable reworking. Molyneux installed the cherry paneling and the beamed ceiling. A Dubuffet hangs over the fireplace; the art deco carpet is by Da Silva.

A detail of the library, with French club chairs from the 1920s. "Very subtly," says the designer, "this room has an art deco theme." The painting is by Dubuffet.

room, as it was consistent with the prewar flavor of the interior. Yet in his choice of lighting he went in a different direction: because there was no place for a single central chandelier, he installed a flexible contemporary fixture. Heading in a different direction still, on the dining area side of the room's long central counter, he commissioned a faux mosaic from Lucretia Moroni. (The pattern is drilled into a layer of acrylic plaster, then painted and sealed.) Based on ancient Roman originals from the Villa Armerina in Sicily, the mosaic is, naturally, partly in ruins.

This confident disregard for period rules or strictures is typical of Molyneux's general approach. In the entry hall, the designer pulled up the battered parquet and installed a faux mosaic floor, again by Moroni, that echoes the artisan's work in the kitchen. This too is in a state of deliberate decay, because "that's how I remember seeing mosaics in Europe," Molyneux explains. "The floor's been walked on for centuries, of course it's not perfect!"

The living room walls were treated with a technique Molyneux used on the parents' living room walls in Palm Beach, called *stucco lucido*; layers of lacquer are applied with a spatula, lending the surface depth and iridescence. "When I first began using *stucco lucido*, it was fairly rare in New York; now you can get it at any paint store," Molyneux observes. In arranging the substantial living room, the designer created two seating areas that are almost exact mirrors of each other—a traditional solution, perhaps, but implemented with furniture that is a mixture of traditional and contemporary. Molyneux combined wicker chairs, a round, English Regency dolphin-base side table, and iron and glass coffee tables by Diego Giacometti. The furniture mediates between the room's neoclassical shell and the more youthful spirit of the art (canvases by Andy Warhol and Robert Rauschenberg) and, of course, of the owners. In a similar juxtaposition, the Corinthian pilasters are joined with a sisal rug, albeit one finished with a Greek key border.

This kind of hybridization prevails in the library too, where an art deco rug is paired with simple Thai tables, and animal prints hang across the room from a Dubuffet that is part of the family's art collection. Here again Molyneux shows his fondness for mixing periods, colors, and patterns. "To make a room interesting, amusing, and alive," the designer says, "it helps to have some vibrancy provoked by an element that shouldn't be there but works all the same." In the case of the library, that element might be the windows, which Molyneux painted a clean, crisp white because they reminded him of the windows in the English school he attended as a boy in Santiago.

Outside the windows, which open onto an air shaft, Molyneux hung a

striped awning and rigged it with lights; a window box beneath gives the illusion of a tiny private garden, particularly at night. With the help of Lucretia Moroni, the designer created a different sort of illusion in the master bedroom. When Molyneux wasn't able to buy a nineteenth-century Agra carpet his client had seen and loved at Sotheby's (he missed the auction), he had it painted on the floor and again in a trompe l'oeil mural in the room's curved entryway. "'You'll never long for that carpet again,' I told her," the designer recalls.

Using furniture, finishes, and textiles here more than structural modifications, Molyneux managed to create interiors that respect, but are not subjugated to, the architecture. In the master bedroom, for instance, trompe l'oeil Gothic arches echo the Gothic details of the building's facade, while the classical pedigree of the living room pilasters is reflected in the ancient Roman torsos and Moroni's faux mosaics. This interplay between past and present is representative of Molyneux's assured and dynamic urban style.

FAR LEFT: The kitchen has a ceramic dining table and chairs copied from originals by Jean Michel Frank. Painting by Rauschenberg.

BELOW: A detail of the master bedroom. A Tiffany lamp stands on the draped table.

CHAPTER FOUR

The Invention of an Interior: Buenos Aires

HIS NEXT PROJECT, an apartment in Buenos Aires, draws on a rigorously architectural facet of Molyneux's talent and training. Presented with the decayed *piano nobile* of the Palacio Ortiz Basualdo, a turn-of-the-century Beaux-Arts mansion in the heart of Buenos Aires, Molyneux faced the interesting challenge of inventing a piece of architecture from the outside in.

From the beginning, there were certain non-negotiable—although not unappealing—constraints. The perimeter of the building, a landmark in the classical French style, could not be modified in any way. The interior would have to live up to the dimensions and grandeur of the exterior, while at the same time remaining in some sort of relationship to its setting. (The French embassy lies to one side and the Brazilian embassy is across the street, both in structures of parallel quality and formal scale.) Then there was the apartment's most conspicuous absence: when the building was converted into separate residences, this particular level was cut off from the grand staircase that formerly connected it to the ground floor and the street beyond, thereby losing both a suitable entrance and a functional and aesthetic focus. Finally, there was the mixed blessing of the apartment's condition, one of severe neglect. All of its original details were gone, which was unfortunate, but this gave Molyneux the freedom to introduce his own.

The client, for whom Molyneux had previously designed an apartment in New York, knew that the designer admired the building, and he asked him to visit it as soon as he acquired the apartment. (He, his wife, and their seven children had been living in the country outside Buenos Aires, but with the older children approaching college age, the parents decided it was time to establish a home in the city.) "Afterward I told him that the only solution I had was a restoration job more than anything else," Molyneux recalls. "The shell was just too important to disregard. Happily, for the building and for me, the client thoroughly agreed."

Much of the apartment was dramatically reconfigured. The spaces were large enough that they could be divided up and still leave rooms of substantial propor-

The gallery's three-quarter columns, marble floor, mirrors, architraves, and moldings were all added by Molyneux, who invested the space with a good deal of neoclassical rigor.

tions. The original floor plan included a music room, two dining rooms of different sizes, a living room, and a salon. Molyneux retained what was necessary for contemporary life (the music room went) and added elements his clients required: six bedrooms and bathrooms, a kitchen, and servants' quarters. During the renovation, which took about two years from start to finish, the apartment was taken down to the cement floors and brick walls, and then it was built up again. "This was a real job, no faux," the designer explains. "Real marble, real stone, real walls."

The craftsmanship is undeniably real, but the project is full of clever examples of architectural legerdemain. Consider the entrance. Molyneux settled on a quintessentially classical solution, a rotunda, which he carved out of existing spaces. On first glance, the room appears to be round, but on closer inspection it is revealed to be square. The viewer's eye is tricked by the colonnade, the domed ceiling, and the marble floor, which is inlaid with a sunburst modeled on the pavement in Michelangelo's Piazza Campidoglio in Rome.

From the rotunda, a visitor next enters the gallery, a similarly classical room that serves as the apartment's central artery or center of distribution. Here, instead of a colonnade, Molyneux installed pairs of three-quarter marble columns. And here too the eye is fooled—this time into believing that the room is wider than it is—by the mirrored panels Molyneux set in between the three-quarter columns. They run from floor to ceiling, with no intervening baseboard or crown molding, and open up the space into complex and elegant reflections. The beams above were gold- and silver-leafed, while the marble floor was laid in a severe geometric pattern. "With all this strong architecture, I decided to use very little furniture, sober furniture," says Molyneux. Sober but also—with Jacob chairs and an eighteenth-century gilded gesso Italian mirror—extremely fine.

Following the perimeter of the building as it does, the apartment's living room presented Molyneux with a quirky and somewhat difficult shape. His first decision was to raise the ceiling, which had been lowered in a previous renovation to a level below the fan lights above the windows. He then applied a large crown molding to conceal the heating and air conditioning ducts that were exposed (and had to be rerouted) as a result. To harmonize with the now significantly higher ceiling, Molyneux added dramatic stone architraves to the doors and, around the circumference of the room, a two-and-a-half-foot baseboard, also of stone, which helped unify the new moldings.

A particular problem was the room's fireplace, which was too small, in the wrong place, and could not be moved. Furthermore, the client had a painting in New York, a Bonnard landscape, rather small itself, that he wanted to hang above the

A corner of the living room: the painting, of classical ruins, is by Giovanni Paolo Pannini. The commode (one of a pair) is eighteenth-century Italian, the chair Regence.

FOLLOWING PAGES:
The eighteenth-century French tapestry depicts the Emperor of China with his astronomers. A late eighteenth-century French desk is paired with a Directoire chair by Jacob; the carpet is nineteenth-century Aubusson.

67

Molyneux solved the problem of
the tiny—and off-center—fireplace
by creating a strongly architectural
surround, rendered in marble to
relate to the gallery next door. The
painting is a Bonnard.

The library is a complete invention of Molyneux's. The paneling is mahogany. The designer found the mantelpiece at an auction in Argentina; its provenance, remarkably, located it as having come from the Palacio Ortiz Basualdo.

mantelpiece. In yet another example of elegant trickery, Molyneux designed a chimney surround that incorporated the wall and the painting. Made of stone and black marble, it echoes the classical patterns of the adjacent gallery and helps bring the fireplace and the luminous canvas into proportion with the rest of the room.

As for furniture, Molyneux combined contemporary sofas, which were his client's request, with such impeccable period pieces as an eighteenth-century French desk, a Jacob chair, a pair of Italian marquetry chests, and a coffee table he designed during his Chilean period. The carpet is Aubusson, and the tapestry—a Molyneux trademark—is eighteenth-century French, in the chinoiserie style.

The library is one of the designer's most ingenious creations, and it's hard to believe that it doesn't date back to the building's earliest inception. Likening the space to the room of a confused magician, Molyneux explains that he made it all up from scratch, out of his own and his client's tastes, interests, and imaginations. Familiar with the client's collection of books, Molyneux devised two levels of mahogany bookshelves, with the upper level reached by a spiral staircase that leads to an elevated corridor. Knowing that his client was fond of mysteries, he created a

LEFT: The library viewed from the staircase that leads to the gallery above.

RIGHT: The dining room furniture is "rather Victorian," says the designer. "I bought the chairs locally. They were described as 'English style,' which sometimes can mean anywhere from William the Conqueror to Elizabeth II!"

74

wall of books that opens when you move a certain volume, revealing a secret passageway into the adjacent dining room; the dining room can also be reached by a more mundane route, by returning to the gallery. Molyneux had a stroke of luck when it came to restoring the fireplace: he found the mantelpiece at auction in Argentina, and its provenance located it as having originally come from the Palacio Ortiz Basualdo! Around the reinstalled fireplace, Molyneux designed a reading nook, and throughout the room he used English Regency furniture, old leather club chairs and sofas, eighteenth-century English portraits, carpet layered upon carpet.

Of all the public rooms, the dining room is probably closest, in size and shape, to the space Molyneux found when he first visited the Palacio Ortiz Basualdo. It has been transformed by the designer's touch, however, with its dramatic tapestry, the antique coffered ceiling Molyneux found hidden behind a plaster ceiling and restored, and the fireplace surround he conceived in a spirit congruent with the one in the living room. In every way, this project was a labor of love for Juan Pablo. "I love the family and the city, and as for the building," he says, "I considered it an honor to be able to bring it back to life."

CHAPTER FIVE

Remaking a Town House on Manhattan's Upper East Side

"THERE ARE OLD PEOPLE who are very nice, and there are old people who aren't very nice," Molyneux believes. "And it's the same with houses. There's no point in keeping mistakes merely because they were made a long time ago."

This complex project on the Upper East Side supports Molyneux's long held thesis that restoration for the sake of restoration is an exercise in design futility. When his clients, a European couple who maintain additional residences outside of New York, took him to visit this late nineteenth-century limestone town house, Molyneux inspected the building carefully. Although the house had been remodeled over the years and was in severe disrepair, it still had period details that another designer might have chosen to restore, struggling to wrest the house's earlier and better incarnation out of its later modifications. Molyneux had the opposite feeling. While many of the rooms may have suited the needs of its occupants in the 1890s, they were useless and repetitive in the 1990s. The kitchen was in the basement. The period elements that were extant were undistinguished. In addition, the clients wanted a swimming pool installed on the roof, which necessitated considerable restructuring. Molyneux told them that the only practical and aesthetic solution was to demolish the interior completely, and they agreed. At one point early in the project, the designer remembers, a visitor would open the front door and see nothing but brick walls and sky overhead.

Molyneux kept only the facade, first because the residence was part of the Upper East Side landmark district but also because he modeled the project on certain European town houses whose plain shells conceal wonderfully elaborate interiors. With this project, Molyneux deliberately sought to counteract a way of life that he sees often in contemporary America, a transient or temporary relationship people have to their environment. "I don't know anyone in New York among my friends who lives in their parents' or grandparents' place, whereas it's just the opposite in Europe. What I imagined for this house was a family that had been rooted for generations."

The irony, of course, is that Molyneux *imagined* this and conceived the house

Installing a swimming pool on the roof of this Upper East Side town house required restructuring the entire building. The mosaic is the real thing, created by visiting craftsmen from Spain.

The entry hall. Faced with low ceilings, bulky columns, and many doors, Molyneux unified the space with a strong but simple marble floor. He fluted the columns to make them appear less massive.

from scratch. His clients made only a few general requests. They wanted a neoclassical living room, a paneled library, and a continental dining room. They expected a level of formality equal to their residences in Europe. They contributed a few paintings to the interiors, but Molyneux supplied most everything else.

He had two inescapable impediments. In order to support the swimming pool on the roof, two steel columns had to run through each floor, from the roof to the basement. Then, given the fixed perimeter of the building, Molyneux could create only two principal rooms per floor, one in front, the other in back, which is customary in New York town houses of a certain scale. "The grander the town house," Molyneux points out, "the simpler it becomes, since you don't want to break up the space you're given." Architecturally, this project was less of a challenge than the Buenos Aires project, where he had almost too much room. Molyneux's solution was to treat each floor as a set of apartments. While the whole of the house expresses a larger relationship, an intimate stylistic rapport was aimed for on each level.

The one exception is the entry, which is the only public space on the ground floor. Here, Molyneux had the additional encumbrance of low ceilings (they're just over eight feet) and, because of the pool, a pair of prominent and rather bulky columns. He fluted them to make them feel lighter, and he marbleized them in order to link them to the real marble staircase and floor, whose simple geometric design set the tone for this crisp, uncluttered space.

Molyneux was able to create a grander hall, or center of distribution, on the living room level. The ceilings rose and could tolerate a more elaborate crown molding; the doors too, were taller, and could support elegant architraves. All moldings were painted to imitate Florentine stone, cool and sober against the warmer *stucco lucido* of the walls. Molyneux left the room intentionally empty: an English Regency table and English Regency griffin stools, all quite formal and architectural, set the tone for the rest of the floor.

The living room, whose three windows face the street, is one of the most formal interiors Molyneux has ever designed. He conceived of it, he says, as "a cocktail room, or a room for after-dinner conversation, very rigorous and very symmetrical." Symmetry, indeed, was key. In this perfectly square space, Molyneux created mirrored arrangements: two sofas, two pairs of English Regency chairs, two nineteenth-century Russian side tables, four Italian wall sconces, and so on. Textiles too, were formal: damasks, silks, and an Aubusson rug.

In the dining room, Molyneux was able to be more inventive architecturally. Though basically rectangular, the town house has an L-shaped extension in back,

LEFT PAGE: The upstairs hall is actually a more suitable introduction to the scale and sensibility of the house. The taller ceilings allowed for more complicated moldings, which conceal stereo speakers and air-conditioning ducts.

FOLLOWING PAGES: The most formal room in the house, the living room is precisely twenty-three feet square, and most of its furniture and objects are neoclassical and paired. The English Regency chaise is the focal point of the interior.

and it was here, on this level, that Molyneux chose to situate the kitchen. But a service hallway was needed for access to the living room—and, of course, there were the two swimming pool columns again. Molyneux's solution was to let the columns frame a niche and to route the service hallway around it. In one stroke, he enlivened the dining room and made the floor efficiently functional.

Because the room was tall, somewhat lacking in interest, and thrown off balance by its single window, Molyneux decided to use somewhat more complicated moldings here. These he painted a sharp white to contrast with the blue lacquered walls, creating a dramatic background for the main table, which is George III (a smaller Regency table stands in the niche and is used for breakfast) and the chairs, which, though English Regency in feeling, are actually late eighteenth-century Russian, as is the chandelier. Molyneux added what is for him an unusually ornate curtain on the window because the room is classically English and grand, and the curtain is typical of such an environment.

The designer relaxed some of the formality as he moved up a level to the library and the master bedroom. The library, which stands over the living room and has a parallel bank of three street-facing windows, is paneled in bird's-eye maple instead of the traditional mahogany one would expect in an English library. Molyneux felt that the lighter wood was in keeping with the relaxed tone of this floor. He conceived of the red, brown, and gold rug, which is his own design, as one of his reversed ceilings: "There isn't that much detailing in the room, so I put the moldings on the floor," Molyneux explains. The furniture, again, is mostly English Regency, with two eighteenth-century German armoires providing bulk and stature. The Prussian war helmets mounted behind the desk reflect the client's interest in military history.

In the master bedroom down the hall, Molyneux continued his red and gold palette, almost as if the bedroom were the sleeping area for a self-contained gentleman's apartment. The bathroom, with its classical moldings and wood paneling, has its own library-like sensibility, and the wood *is* mahogany here.

Molyneux continued his apartment approach on the next floor, with the elegant sitting room and bedroom in suite. Because of the drop in ceilings, Molyneux used simpler moldings, but he compensated for the diminution of architecture by heightening the palette, using generous amounts of red, green, and gold, which he drew from an eighteenth-century Japanese screen. This room, and the adjacent bedroom, have a Brighton Pavilion gaiety about them, a tone set in part by the fanciful eighteenth-century English bed.

Similarly, the two guest bedrooms upstairs share a tonal and stylistic

LEFT: The dining room's round niche allowed Molyneux to create two seating areas.

ABOVE: The view into the upstairs hall creates a sense of continuing space.

LEFT: The library furniture is a lively combination of styles and periods. Molyneux has combined German armoires, eighteenth-century Russian chairs, a French cabinet, and an English Regency desk.

ABOVE: Behind the desk, Molyneux mounted the client's collection of mostly Prussian war helmets, which reflect his interest in military history.

RIGHT: A drawing of the library rug, which Molyneux designed after classical moldings.

BELOW AND FAR RIGHT: The master bathroom, where mahogany columns open up to reveal medicine cabinets.

The upstairs sitting room features a Japanese lacquer table and six-panel screen, which was part of the client's collection. The chairs in the foreground are eighteenth-century French.

relationship. Molyneux's inspiration for the moss green in one bedroom was a hotel suite at Claridge's. To add character to the room's still lower ceilings and less architectural detailing, Molyneux designed bowed and peaked valances for the curtains and a patterned woven rug for the floor.

The house's *pièce de résistance*—and engineering feat—is the swimming pool, which had to be lifted into place by a crane. The classical mosaic was installed by Spanish craftsmen, who worked on it over a period of several months. The bold panels of Valentino fabric conceal a television and a music system. There is an adjoining dressing room and bath, and the glass ceiling can be opened up to the sky.

Each floor of this ambitious house may feel like its own contained, highly elegant apartment, but the sum reflects a clear relationship among the individual parts. In terms of the level of detailing, the generally restrained use of color, and the formality and quality of the furniture, this is unquestionably a single residence. Only the pool, on first impression, seems to be a fantasy unto itself, but its mosaic and statuary are as classical in their way as the architraves downstairs. "I loved the challenge of the whole project, which is as big an architectural job as I've done in New York," Molyneux says by way of summary, "but I particularly welcomed the challenge of the pool. It affected every element in the house's design, but it was worth it in the end."

LEFT: An eighteenth-century Aubusson carpet sets a rich tone for the master bedroom. The bed, also eighteenth-century, is English.

BELOW: A design for the swimming pool mosaic, seen on page 96–97.

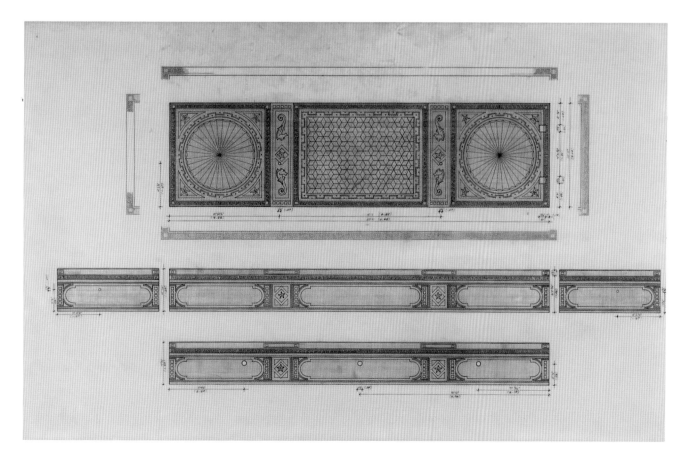

ABOVE: A hall leading from the library to the master bedroom; its neoclassical marble flooring links the space to other common areas in the house. The wall panels are eighteenth-century Chinese.

RIGHT: Molyneux employed a subdued moss green palette in the guest room. The furniture is a mix of English, French, and Swedish pieces.

The pool being lowered onto the roof (above) and (right) ready for laps. The marble fountain (outside, on the terrace) and the statue of Mars, both English, are in the classical manner.

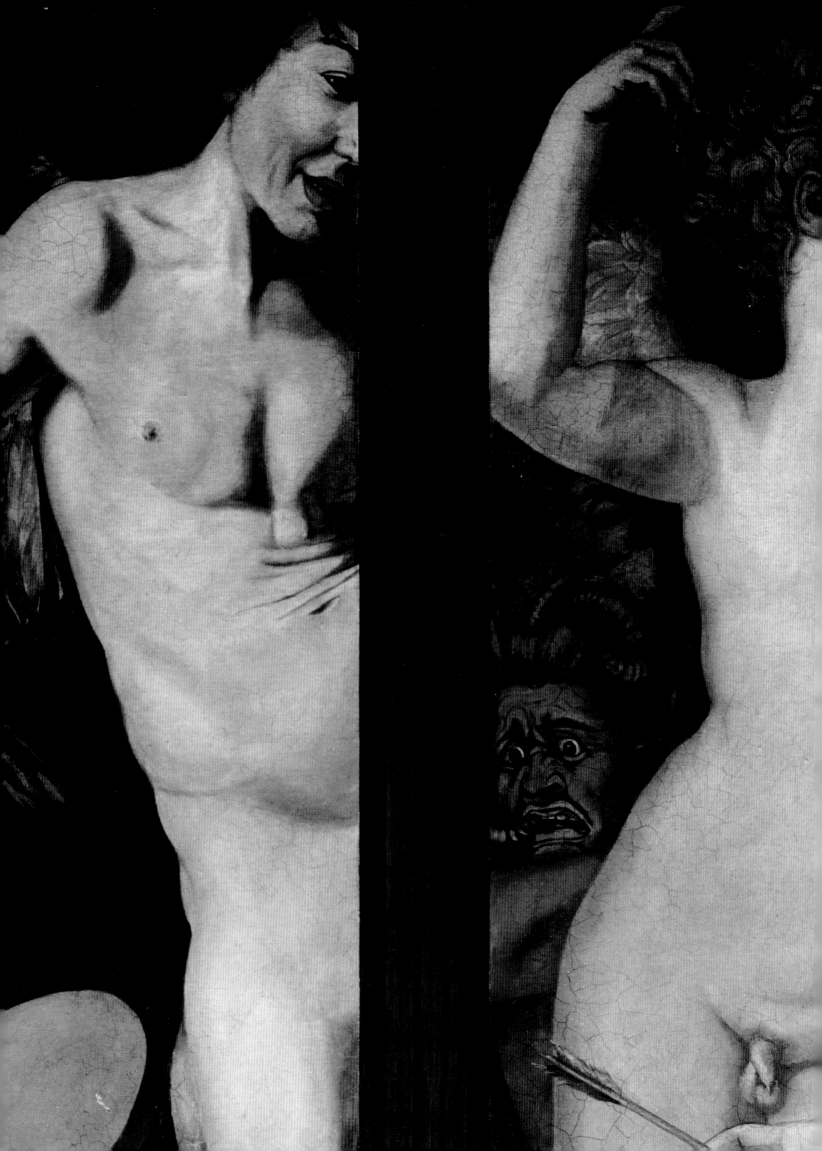

CHAPTER SIX

Molyneux at Home

I. NEW YORK

ALL HIS LIFE Juan Pablo Molyneux has been in the habit of living and working in the same building, and in the mid-1980s, when he moved to New York from Buenos Aires, he continued this tradition. During his first few years in America, Molyneux was still traveling back and forth between Buenos Aires and New York. His wife, Pilar, came and went as well, so Juan Pablo was able to make do with the rented piano nobile of an Upper East Side town house. Eventually, however, as he spent more and more time in the States, he began to cast about for more permanent quarters. It was actually Pilar who found them. "She was new to the city," Molyneux recalls, "and she had the idea that we should put an ad in the paper saying exactly what we were looking for. It seemed like a long shot to me, but, remarkably, the next day we received a call from the owner of this place."

This was in 1987. For the first few years, Molyneux rented two floors in the handsome neoclassical French town house on 69th Street. Gradually he took over more rooms, and he bought the building outright in 1989. The town house, which is twenty-two feet wide and made of limestone, was built in the late nineteenth century and consists of seven floors in all. It was in good shape when Molyneux acquired it, although he has reconfigured or adapted many of the floors to suit his very specific mixture of personal and professional needs.

Initially, the ground-level entry was divided into a lobby and a hall that led to a rented office behind. Molyneux removed the dividing wall and painted the enlarged space in a mixture of terra cotta and faux stone. He retained the fireplace, changed the lighting fixtures, and had the elevator fitted with old master panels after Caravaggio. His goal for the room was "elegant but open and simple," the designer explains. "It gets a lot of traffic, and then, of course, I needed a place to garage my motorcycles." One or more of the Harley-Davidsons that Molyneux designed in 1995 is always parked in the lobby, where it looks like a piece of modern sculpture set against this vivid Italianate background.

From the ground-floor entry, a visitor can proceed to the official entrance

LEFT: Panels after Caravaggio by Anne Harris enliven the elevator.

FOLLOWING PAGES: Molyneux's office, with its four work areas and more than a dozen shades of (deliberately mismatched) red.

of the J. P. Molyneux studio, where a receptionist works in an anteroom. Beyond, there is a large white room divided into various work stations: bookkeeping desks, storage for fabric samples, and drafting tables. Molyneux's intention was to create an extremely simple, even blank, background, so there would be no competition with the design work and drafting that takes place here.

He took a parallel approach on the floor above, which can be reached by way of a spiral staircase linking the downstairs workroom to its sibling upstairs, or else by way of a staircase that leads from the lobby to a foyer on the piano nobile. This is the route clients take when they come to see Molyneux in his office.

Molyneux insists on an open approach in his work environment. From the foyer, a visitor can see into the large workroom, which the designer has arrayed simply

with a pair of pine columns; drafting tables, naturally; and, on the mantelpiece, a group from his collection of Chinese zodiac figures. This room replaces the town house's original dining room and kitchen and has handsome period moldings, which Molyneux has painted white. On the opposite side of the foyer is Molyneux's office, which occupies the former living room.

Clients often move back and forth between Molyneux's office and the work-room. "People love to be seated in an architect's chair," he explains. "They look at pictures and sketch things themselves. This is the way I measure how much they understand of a project. I used to keep the environment very clean and ordered, but now I don't mind if there are samples and other materials out. Reasonable disorder," he says, "can be surprisingly stimulating."

LEFT: At work in the drafting areas: Molyneux (right) with colleagues Johannes Grobler (left) and Harald Heissmann (center).

RIGHT: Chinese zodiac figures guard over plans in progress.

The library upstairs features a
Gothic-style stone mantelpiece and
paneling that were salvaged from a
now-forgotten nineteenth-century
house. The seventeenth-century
Coromandel screen depicts objects
belonging to a collector. The
still life over the fireplace is by
Margherita Caffi.

Unlike the drafting room, Molyneux's office is highly designed—and vividly too, since it contains almost a dozen deliberately mismatched shades of red, his favorite color. The room retains its original crown moldings, nineteenth-century French marble fireplace, and parquet floor, although Molyneux enlarged the opening and installed mahogany French doors. (These are fitted with one-way glass, so that his assistants can see if he is on the phone or in the middle of a conversation.) Molyneux designed bookshelves and a baseboard out of the same burnished mahogany and re-created the ceiling from his 1991 Kips Bay room (see Chapter Twelve), with its trompe l'oeil canvas by Anne Harris. He upholstered the walls in a red-and-white stripe pattern and gilded the existing mirror over the fireplace.

In addition to a sitting area, the office has four distinct work areas: Molyneux's main desk, which is an eighteenth-century English architect's table; a smaller campaign desk in the window, where he likes to read in the bright natural daylight; a third marble-topped desk, another Kips Bay holdover (1985), whose ample surface is good for spreading out papers; and, finally, a large, round, tapestry-covered conference table surrounded by Regency armchairs, where he often meets with clients. The office is capable of metamorphosing too. When Juan Pablo and Pilar give large dinner parties,

FAR LEFT: A detail of the dining room. An early nineteenth-century Japanese screen stands in the background.

LEFT: The unusual melon-shaped commode in the master bedroom is eighteenth-century Italian.

BELOW: A detail of the master bedroom with painted silk pillows after Michelangelo.

the sofa goes into the lobby downstairs, his desk pivots and is pushed up against the wall, and two mates to the conference table come out of storage and are set up, enabling the couple to seat thirty comfortably.

On the floor above Molyneux's office is the library, whose neo-Gothic chestnut paneling and stone fireplace Molyneux speculates were probably salvaged from a nineteenth-century European house and transported here. Originally, the room had another, later set of bookshelves, which Molyneux removed, installing a seventeenth-century Coromandel screen in their place. He painted a trompe l'oeil sky on the ceiling partly to open up the room but partly to mask its uneven plasterwork. The interior is intensely personal, with a Turkish rug he found at auction near his house in the Berkshires, a piece of tapestry and a pair of eighteenth-century French *bibliothèques* from his mother's house, and the Anglo-Afghan chairs from the red library he designed for the 1985 Kips Bay show house.

Across the hall from the library is the master bedroom, which Molyneux upholstered in a silver damask. The bed's canopy conceals a television projector, and a screen lowers over the fireplace. An unusual melon-shaped Italian commode and a Dutch marquetry cabinet are among the more striking pieces of antique furniture. The room is serene and understated, but Molyneux admits that Pilar wants a yellow room next time. "It's fine with me," says the designer. "I'm always looking forward to a new project." Indeed, as he travels through his house, Molyneux imagines painting the library, creating a new dining room, and redoing the guest rooms, which occupy the floors above.

The only absolute constants in Molyneux's private quarters are his gym and dressing room on the top floor and the terrace, with its continuous-lap pool, pergola, and ample seating. "It's weird to imagine that you are in New York when you're up here," Molyneux says. "It's so lush and fragrant. And inviting—which is important. When you live and work at home, sometimes you need a place to escape."

ABOVE: Molyneux's exercise room.

RIGHT: The rooftop, with its continuous-lap pool.

2. COUNTRY

O N WEEKENDS, Juan Pablo and Pilar escape in a different and more complete
way to their country house, a 1782 wood-frame structure in western Massachusetts.
They came across the property quite by accident: the couple had been spending their
weekends in the Hamptons and were looking for a place to buy there when, after
having "one of those nightmare traffic experiences" familiar to many Hamptons-
bound New Yorkers, Juan Pablo decided he would never visit the popular beach towns
again—at least on a regular basis. A friend sent him a Polaroid of this property in
the Berkshires, and he decided to investigate the following Saturday.

"I'd never been to the Berkshires before," Molyneux remembers, "but I
instantly fell in love with the house and the setting." The setting, fifty acres of flatlands
with access to eighty acres of woods, was tranquil and lush. The house, a solid example of Federal architecture, was listed on the National Register of Historic Places. It
had been continuously occupied by the original family, the Buells, and was intact
architecturally, although in a state of some disrepair. The last Buell, an elderly woman
of ninety-five, had died five years earlier, and the house had not been occupied since.

Molyneux leapt at the chance to restore the property and make it over according to his own principles. This meant, of course, salvaging the house's successful elements, modifying its mistakes, modernizing the amenities, and bringing what the
designer calls a "somewhat broader approach" to bear on the interiors.

The house required a good deal of structural repair. Heating and plumbing
were replaced, as were the old windows, although, of course, with exact copies of
the originals. The entire structure was re-roofed, and the foundation—which was,
interestingly, built of marble—was jacked up and made level again. Downstairs,
Molyneux limited his reconfiguring to adding a piece of the central hallway to the
library. Upstairs, he created a master suite out of three tiny bedrooms and a guest
bedroom out of former servants' quarters. The house now has four bedrooms in all,
a library, a kitchen, a dining room, a living room, and a morning room.

"I didn't want to do a rustic American house," the designer explains. "For
one thing, I have no Shaker grandmother, and for another, people traveled in the
eighteenth century and brought all kinds of sophisticated furniture, paintings, and
objects back with them." Another precedent Molyneux had in mind was the nineteenth-
century invasion of the Berkshires by the new rich, whose elaborate "cottages" were

The designer and his wife often
dine *à deux* in the library. The
Continental tapestry is seventeenth-
century and on the naïve side;
"It's almost cartoonish," says
Molyneux, "which somehow
suits the country."

On the left is Goodwood, Molyneux's country house in western Massachusetts; built in 1782 and enlarged over the years, it is a fine example of rural Federal architecture. The caretaker's house in the center is nineteenth-century. The small structure to the right, a former chicken coop, has been converted into a tennis house; it contains a sauna.

filled with European furniture and decorations—albeit not always of the finest quality.

Molyneux was fortunately able to buy some of the Buells' furniture at an auction of the house's contents. Among his acquisitions was an American Empire sofa that became the cynosure of the entry hall. Molyneux set it against a document wallpaper, a reproduction of an eighteenth-century French pattern of birds and flowers on a vivid yellow background. "It's probably a more sophisticated paper than the house would have had originally," the designer explains, "but I saw nothing wrong with imagining a cosmopolitan flavor for this room."

The living room was a particularly fine example of sophisticated Federal architecture in the rural manner—so fine, in fact, that a prominent museum was negotiating for its acquisition before Molyneux bought the house. The crown moldings, door and window surrounds, and fireplace were all intact; Molyneux painted them a subdued gray (a color he calls "elephant") and paired them with a replica of an eighteenth-century damask that was initially made for a rural house in the south of France. Molyneux's calibration toward the rural is loosened up somewhat in his choice of furnishings, which include a Knole sofa, a pair of George III armchairs,

The books in the library belonged to Ambassador Buell, one of the house's former owners; they date from the 1930s and mostly concern foreign affairs. The writing table is English Regency.

ABOVE: The living room has a handsome set of Federal moldings, once sought by a prominent American museum. The rug is eighteenth-century Aubusson.

RIGHT: Molyneux created the guest room by joining two servants' bedrooms, raising and installing a tray ceiling, and adding two new windows.

and an eighteenth-century Aubusson rug.

In enlarging the library, Molyneux was fortunately able to match its paneling and molding by salvaging and adapting the house's attic floor. He had the pine boards cut and stained to continue the line of the room. In the original house, which had been added to in the nineteenth century, the library was the kitchen, hence the substantial stone cooking fireplace that now anchors one end of the much-expanded room. The bookshelves were in place when Molyneux bought the house, and so were the books, which he acquired at the Buell auction. Molyneux selected a Portuguese needlepoint rug, a reproduction of an English Regency design, for its library-like greens, browns, and reds. Most of the furniture is English and eighteenth-century and continues the gentlemanly mood of the interior.

The dining room's blue and white palette was influenced by the dining room Molyneux designed for Kips Bay in 1988 (see Chapter Twelve). The rug, in fact, comes *from* that interior, whereas the Chinese zodiac figures, part of the set Molyneux keeps in his office, were loaned to it.

In the dining room, Molyneux used a vibrant toile de Jouy, which he chose for the country feeling conveyed by the proliferation of flora and fauna. He purchased the nineteenth-century New York table locally and acquired the Victorian chairs, again, from the Buell auction. The rug was recycled from his 1988 Kips Bay dining room, while the Chinese zodiac figures were loaned to it (see Chapter Twelve).

The master bedroom belongs to a suite Molyneux fashioned out of three tinier bedrooms. For the walls, the bed, and the curtains, he used a hand-printed linen from Portugal, chosen for its country sensibility. Similarly, in the guest room that was made out of the former servants' quarters, Molyneux used another pastoral toile. "These serene but joyful patterns seem very fitting to me in the country," the designer says. "It's appropriate to keep a sense of the outdoors in a setting where you spend so much time, as Pilar and I do, riding, swimming, playing tennis, and gardening."

ABOVE: An exterior view of the caretaker's house.

LEFT: "The linen's leaves and flowers lend the space a wonderful country feeling," Molyneux says of the master bedroom. The fabric was made in Portugal.

123

3. VAIL

*M*OLYNEUX GREW UP SKIING and has always been fond of the mountains. In 1992, he and a school friend jointly acquired a house in Vail, Colorado, which they use separately many weeks during the winter and a few during the summer as well.

The original house was undistinguished. Built in the 1960s, it was vaguely chalet-like in design, with a stone foundation and wood siding. It had, Molyneux recalls, no real architecture to speak of, and in planning his renovation he never intended to turn it into something it could never be. "It was an extremely poor house," the designer says. "I wanted to go from poor to decent, and out of this decent architecture, I wanted to make a comfortable home and one that responded to the setting and the particular needs of the people using it."

Although Molyneux is a joint owner of the house, his partner, logically enough, left him in charge of its remodeling and interior design. Working for himself, Molyneux says, allowed him to go at his own speed—which is fast—and to add several elements that were missing from the original structure.

The first was a proper entrance, which is always important to Molyneux. Formerly, a visitor walked into a tiny corridor, where there was an impractical spiral staircase leading to the second floor. Molyneux designed a new double-height entry hall and a traditional staircase. He selected materials that were simple, informal, and appropriate to the mountain setting: pine for the bannister, beams, timbering, and molding; Mexican stone and black slate for the checkerboard floor; and a woolen carpet mimicking deer hide on the staircase.

He dramatically reconfigured the second floor, which contains the house's common rooms. The former living room became the library, which Molyneux opened up to a single room on the third floor, linking it by means of the salvaged and recycled spiral staircase. This choice admitted more light into the library and created a work area for Molyneux to set up a drafting table. He paneled the library and workroom in more pine, enlarged the windows, and created an entertainment center. He left the stone fireplace, which was original to the house and one of its better features.

Molyneux created the new living room out of the former master bedroom and several terraces, which he enclosed. His materials here too, were simple: pine ceiling and beams, Chinese slate for the floor and fireplace. He added a pine wainscoting

An exterior view of Molyneux's red house in Vail, where he is an avid and frequent skier.

to help bring the room, which has a steep pitch, into better proportion.

"In a house you don't live in all year round, you don't get bored with things," Molyneux observes. It was this idea, together with the mountain setting, that influenced his choice of animal hides, heads, and imagery; horn chairs and tables; and various primitive textiles and decorative objects that are drawn from a range of different cultures and include eighteenth-century Russian horse blankets, Moroccan pottery lamp bases, and Turkish kilim rugs. These objects may come from different ends of the world, but they have certain qualities in common: they are handmade from natural materials and are often bold, geometric, and intensely colored. "You can bring together all kinds of different things if you keep in mind the geography of a place, its function, and the mood you want to achieve," Molyneux says. "Silks and taffetas would be absurd in the mountains, as would highly polished English or gilded French furniture."

ABOVE: The sofas, a Molyneux design, have cut corners to accomodate the traffic paths in the room; the coffee table is made out of a section of antique parquet floor.

LEFT: The designer added the entry hall to the house, which was originally built in the 1960s. Navajo rugs and a Native American ceremonial buffalo skin set a primitive tone.

ABOVE: Eighteenth-century Russian horse blankets enliven a corner of the living room.

LEFT: The house's original living room was only a quarter of its present size; the paintings are by Ronaldo de Juan. The antler chairs were made in Colorado.

FAR LEFT: Another corner of the living room, with a table made out of horns. "The mountains are the one place where you can use this kind of furniture," Molyneux says. "It reminds you of where you are."

LEFT: The eighteenth-century Russian shawls on the bed and floor of the master bedroom were originally part of wedding trousseaus for Georgian brides.

The dining room seems, at first glance, to be something of a departure, with its nineteenth-century French tapestry, its suite of Regency chairs, and the pair of fluted columns that serve as a base for the table. "But the subject of the tapestry is pastoral," Molyneux points out, "and the chairs are made of pewter, and while the columns may be classical, they are carved out of rough stone and they support a rustic slab of wood."

In two master bedrooms of roughly equal size, Molyneux collected several pieces of painted Tyrollean furniture, which comes from the Alps and is handcrafted, like many of the other objects in the house. "In this setting," he says, "it's entirely appropriate." Molyneux has, once again, allowed setting to inform his interiors. In Vail, as in New York and the Berkshires, location and landscape are critical influences on the designer's work.

Molyneux ordered the ready-made stone columns from Mexico and had a local carpenter make the rustic wooden tabletop. The tapestry is nineteenth-century French.

132

CHAPTER SEVEN

Transforming an Apartment on Park Avenue

O CCASIONALLY, Molyneux will be approached by a client who asks him to reproduce a version of something he has created before. In the case of the redesign of this Park Avenue apartment, Molyneux's client had seen his work in the Palacio Ortiz Basualdo in Buenos Aires (see Chapter Four) and was particularly impressed with its entrance gallery—so impressed, in fact, that he set out to buy an apartment in New York with a suitable long narrow hall that could be treated in a similar architectural manner.

The apartment he found, a sprawling prewar unit on Manhattan's Upper East Side, had the necessary hall but not much else to recommend it. Ten years earlier, the interiors had been given a very contemporary treatment. They had been stripped of their moldings and other detailing and were virtually without character. Other than the hall, the floor plan did not meet the clients' needs; they were a retired couple and had little use for its five modest bedrooms. The task before Molyneux was to transform the contemporary into the neoclassical and find a better use for the square footage from the superfluous bedrooms.

This apartment is, in many ways, about its two galleries: the entrance gallery and the gallery Molyneux created for the husband's bath. Formerly a plain rectangle, the entrance gallery received some of the designer's most rigorous architectural detailing and is indeed very much in the spirit of its Buenos Aires sibling. The ceiling has been spanned with beams that conceal air-conditioning ducts, the walls are lined with three-quarter columns, and the mahogany doors are set within strong pediments. Moldings are generous and gilded. The plaster columns have been given a trompe l'oeil marble finish, a lighter and more playful contrast to the real marble floor, which is set in a geometric design. Molyneux has kept the furniture to a minimum: an English George III gilded console table, which he chose for the ornate note it lends to the room and the way its marble top integrates with the floor; a pair of blue and white Chinese vases; and, from the clients' existing art collection, a Larry Rivers canvas and a sculpture of the Venus di Milo by Jim Dine.

The apartment's second "gallery" is somewhat more unexpected. Molyneux

The classic—and neoclassical—Molyneux entry hall features a colonnade of three-quarter columns, a beamed ceiling, pediments over the doors, and a geometric marble floor. The ceiling mural is by Anne Harris.

The master bathroom is the apartment's second gallery. The cabinetry is mahogany, the surfaces a combination of real and faux marble.

RIGHT: Another detail of the master bath.

FAR RIGHT: The husband's combined study-and-dressing-room. The barometer is nineteenth-century English.

took the space from two-and-a-half of the extra bedrooms and turned it into the husband's striking bathroom. He created, in effect, a colonnade framing a series of niches and inserted the functions of the bathroom into each niche. One contains the sink, another the toilet, a third a walk-in shower, with exercise equipment filling a fourth. The bathtub anchors the far end of the gallery, while doors leading to a small private library are opposite it. (This room is accessible only from the bathroom and contains a television and breakfast table.) Throughout the bathroom, the green and white marble is real up to the point that it can be touched; beyond that it is painted. All the woodwork is mahogany, as is the eighteenth-century Chippendale settee.

The remainder of the apartment's public rooms are almost modest by comparison. Molyneux further banished the apartment's contemporary pedigree by adding moldings to the living room and moldings and beams to the dining room. He upholstered the walls of both rooms with damask, in light tones at his clients' request. Yellows, creams, and beiges prevail throughout the interiors, although there is a characteristic touch of Molyneux red, especially in the chinoiserie secretary in the living room.

This piece of furniture comes with an interesting story. After searching fruitlessly for a red lacquered bureau bookcase, Molyneux convinced the client to buy one at auction that was in poor shape. He tackled it as if it were a room: he stripped off the old black lacquer; he changed the feet, which had been replaced; he added a

Anne Harris painted the dining room ceiling panels. Inspired by Tiepolo, they depict the four continents.

pediment and interior fittings, both of which were missing; and he had the finished piece relacquered in red and gold. "When we put it together, it looked quite amazing," says the designer, "and it turned out to be a much more fun way to go."

Molyneux's curtaining in this apartment is more elaborate than is his usual style. This was partly in response to the wife's request but partly because, in the living room and dining room at least, the architecture was minimal, and he felt the rooms could benefit from the more intricate drapery. "If you take away the moldings and the curtains," he explains, "you're pretty much left with a plain box."

He selected an even more complicated crown molding for the master bedroom, which is upholstered in cotton damask and fitted with a wall-to-wall needlepoint rug. The eighteenth-century crown over the bed contributes an architectural detail of its own; gilded and curved, it introduces a bit of flash to the otherwise linear, subdued space.

"This apartment is an intriguing combination," Molyneux says in retrospect. "There are areas that required a lot of architectural detailing and others that are, in their way, rather simple. The combination of the two strikes a good balance. Not every room can sustain a grand colonnade, after all!"

ABOVE: Molyneux added the molding to the master bedroom but dropped it to accommodate cove lighting.

LEFT: The living room's buoyant palette was derived from the 1920s Aubusson rug. "For some reason, it makes me think of Cannes," says the designer.

CHAPTER EIGHT

A Bicultural Journey in Laguna Beach

A DESIGNER AS RESTLESS as Juan Pablo Molyneux is seldom content to go on repeating his past successes, even when he is specifically asked to do so by a client. Such was the case with the owners of this 13,000-square-foot house on a hillside above the Pacific in Laguna Beach, California. Familiar with Molyneux's work, they approached him with the idea of commissioning one of his representative European neoclassical interiors. When the designer visited them in the interim house they were renting in the area, however, he had a different idea. The couple, who are both Syrian, had surrounded themselves with silver, textiles, and several pieces of furniture from their native country. Intrigued by these objects, Molyneux immediately suggested combining the Damascene with the neoclassical and creating a house that merged the two aesthetics. "The clients were a little hesitant at first," Molyneux recalls. "But I felt that the potential was immense, and I managed to persuade them to let me go off in a new direction."

Molyneux began by studying Damascene decorative arts, which are characterized by intricate filigreed motifs, whether executed in metal, wood, or on the loom. Damascene woodwork is often carved, inlaid, and gilded, while Damascene textiles are dense and highly patterned—the word "damask," in fact, comes from Damascus, where these fine silk fabrics were made in the Middle Ages and were introduced to Europe in the eleventh century. Before work on the house was begun, the designer traveled to Syria with his clients and made a thorough tour of museums, antique and furniture dealers, textile makers, marble yards, and open markets, buying and commissioning a wide range of furniture, paneling, fabric, and flooring as he went.

Molyneux realized that an all-Damascene house would look out of place in California and also run the danger of seeming—at least in the West—"a little heavy-handed." Mostly, he explains, this was because of the liberal use of new gold in Syrian decorative arts. His solution here, as throughout the house, was to introduce certain European elements, from old, faded gold fabrics to sober Ionic columns to pieces of highly architectural French furniture. "I thought of the house as southern," Molyneux

The gallery is perhaps the most purely Syrian room in the house. Molyneux commissioned the paneling and the marble floor in Damascus; furniture and lighting fixtures are also Damascene.

says, "though I never specified *which* southern. It could be in the south of France or Italy or Cypress, or, indeed, in Southern California."

Molyneux came on the scene after the floor plans had been drawn by a local architect and a building permit issued. Retaining the footprint of the house, he proceeded to make certain modifications and additions, among them a typical Molyneux gallery (or center of distribution), hall, and rotunda. These spaces may have been typical Molyneux in floor plan and function, but the designer treated them to the same cross-cultural fertilizing that characterizes the entire house. The rotunda is actually an outdoor terrace that faces the sea, yet allows access to the gallery, the living room, and the library, very much as an interior rotunda might. The gallery is fitted with paneling, marble, and furniture made in Damascus, while the adjoining hall is more European in flavor. The motifs in its marble floor, for example, though still in the same combination of yellow, brown, and white Molyneux used in the gallery, become more French and less Islamic; the chair railing, while remaining at the same height, becomes simpler and more neoclassical; and pairs of Ionic columns frame the doors. "Instead of clashing," Molyneux says, "this mixture is, I think, a kind of journey between two cultures."

ABOVE AND LEFT: In the living room, Molyneux carefully integrated the newer and more vivid gold hues of the Syrian fabrics with the older, more faded gold of the crown molding, the Italian wall fabric, and the French Empire armchairs.

FOLLOWING PAGES: The dining room viewed from two angles. The nineteenth-century green glass chandelier is English. The French table is surrounded by Swedish chairs; all are nineteenth-century.

Molyneux found the seventeenth-century niches in Damascus. Made of carved, painted, and gilded wood and glass, they depict windows set among intricate columns, swags, and curtains. The Syrian silver is from the clients' collection.

NEAR RIGHT AND BELOW:
The plan for, and realization of,
the master bedroom floor, which
has inserts of lapis lazuli set into
the parquet.

FAR RIGHT: Molyneux's "Syrian-
Swedish" master bedroom unites
a Swedish chandelier and suite of
chairs with a Syrian table.

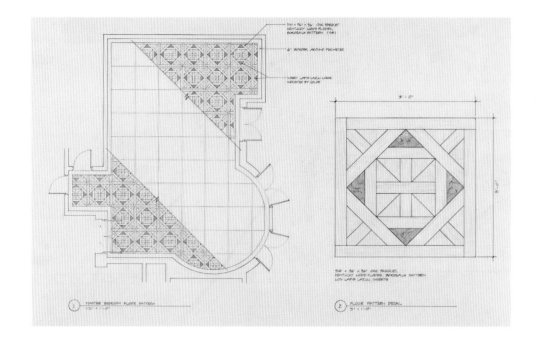

The journey continues in the house's public rooms. In the living room and dining room, Molyneux paired, for the shell, a plain white marble floor and a neoclassical palmetto crown molding. In the living room he then combined Fortuny cotton (on the walls) and Syrian silk (for the curtains) with an English mantelpiece, French Empire armchairs, Swedish stools, and a Chinese coffee table. This confident international approach continues in the dining room, where the fabrics, again, are both Italian and Damascene, the table French, the chairs Swedish, and the dramatic architectural niches seventeenth-century Syrian. Molyneux found these during his visit to Damascus and considers them among the most unusual elements in the house.

"I wonder if the day will come when I'm *not* asked to do an English library," Molyneux observes with a laugh at the space that, more than any other in this project, resembles interiors Molyneux has created elsewhere. The paneling is mahogany, the

LEFT: The pool's marble, like many of the house's materials, comes from Syria.

FAR LEFT: With its mahogany walls and moldings, parquet floor, and bookshelves with marble trim, the library is the most purely European room in the house. The desk is French Empire and has ormolu appliques.

floor parquet, the furniture Empire—yet not entirely: a few Syrian chairs link the room to the rest of the house.

A variant cultural journey characterizes the master bedroom, which Molyneux calls "Syrian Swedish." Here he has matched an eighteenth-century Swedish chandelier and suite of chairs with a Syrian mirror and coffee table. Italian painted panels enliven the elegant, sober room, whose floor has inserts of lapis lazuli embedded in the parquet.

The project took two years to complete and is one of the designer's favorites. "It gave me a chance to stretch and to learn," he observes. "And stretching is good. In fact, it's essential. The eye—and the mind—must always be expanding."

CHAPTER NINE

Vail Revisited

S OMETIMES LIMITATIONS can prod a designer toward innovative solutions, and sometimes these solutions transcend the problem they set out to solve and take the designer's work in a fresh direction. Such was the case with one of Molyneux's most recent projects, the interiors of a 4,800-square-foot house on Mill Creek Circle in Vail.

Mill Creek Circle is one of the ski resort's prime locations, situated as it is next to the main chair lift. Molyneux's clients valued their land but not their house, which was built in the 1960s when Vail was first developed and was architecturally unremarkable. Their initial impulse was to tear the house down and commission an entirely new one, but local building codes have become more rigorous in recent years, and the owners would have been forced to set a new structure farther back on the property, which would have meant losing their view of the ski mountain. In addition, they would have had to reduce their square footage, which they found undesirable. Their solution was to hire Snowdown Hopkins, a local architecture firm, to create a new house on the old foundation.

When Molyneux came on the scene he recognized that the idiosyncratic shape of the blueprint—more or less two rectangles colliding at an odd angle—was a given, as were the sloping ceilings and modestly sized kitchen. The architect had supplied large handsome windows that were well placed to take advantage of the views, and it was from one of these, an exaggerated half-round window divided into four panes of glass, that Molyneux took his first cue in organizing the interiors. A visitor formerly entered directly into the dining room, an approach that Molyneux, with his insistence on well-defined entry halls, disliked intensely. He reduced the dining room and created a narrow hall alongside it. On top of the dividing wall he then extended—actually, intersected—the architect's half-round window with an interior quarter-round window in the same proportions. The solution to the problem feels both seamless and particularly imaginative.

Molyneux treated the new space as part dining room, part library. He paneled

A view from the living room into the combined dining room-library. Different shades of *stucco lucido* help define the spaces.

RIGHT: A whimsical folk art coat rack.

FAR RIGHT: The dining area, with chairs by David Linley and *Autumn Trees* by Georgia O'Keeffe.

the walls with pine up to the bottom of the windows; beyond he applied *stucco lucido* in a strong blue, its dark tone nicely offsetting the intense reflected light from the snow-blanketed mountain. He complicated the pine walls with built-in bookshelves and columns whose fluting and capitals are actually thin linear encrustations of oxidized copper. The furniture here, as throughout the house, is eclectic but with a sensitivity to the Rocky Mountain setting: rustic materials and primitive patterns predominate, as in the American grain-painted blanket chest, the kilim rug, and the Native American baskets. The chairs, which were made by David Linley, have what Molyneux calls "an almost Tyrollean spirit."

Molyneux continued his use of *stucco lucido* in the living room, although he changed from blue to yellow in order to suggest a separation of space between the otherwise open rooms. Here too, he added pine, in the form of carved (and purely decorative) beams, window casings, and the handrail on the staircase. Other rustic materials include the slate floor and the fireplace made of Arizona stone.

Although Molyneux does not object to the kitchen in an informal house being open to the living room, he did anticipate occasions when his clients might like to have some separation between the two rooms, and so he "commissioned" a large Georgia O'Keeffe sunflower from trompe l'oeil artist Anne Harris and mounted it on a motorized panel that closes off the kitchen at the flick of a switch.

While the living room has its share of primitive furnishings, among them a nineteenth-century Indian rug, a Spanish colonial table, and a coffee table made out of a Nepalese window shutter, Molyneux added a refined note in the eighteenth-century

160

FAR LEFT: The view into the living room. The brackets that support the rustic beams are made of steel and follow a random curve: "I imagined a piece of torn paper," says the designer.

LEFT: A detail of the wrought iron banister, which imitates twigs.

BELOW: The television, which is built into in the fireplace.

pine eagle console. It is refined and yet not inconsistent with the mood of the room, particularly now that Molyneux has stripped away its gilding and replaced the marble top with a randomly curving slab of koa. "I took a very fancy piece of furniture down several levels," Molyneux says. "I like the fact that it's hard to tell exactly what it is now."

Molyneux divided the living room furniture into two groupings. The central arrangement is oriented to the fireplace (and television, which is hidden in the chimney); behind it, a second arrangement is anchored by a Thai daybed covered in kilims, as are the pair of ample club chairs nearby. The single open living room-dining room is now broken into three separate arrangements that nonetheless flow together effortlessly during large parties.

Also on the main floor is the master bedroom, where Molyneux created what he calls a "tepee effect" in his beamwork on the ceiling. More kilims continue the primitive vocabulary, as do the Native American sand rug, prints, and dolls. The walls are covered in linen, and in a niche Molyneux set up an adjoining home office.

This was a project, Molyneux explains, where "at first I felt there were quite a few impediments. But the more I thought about it, the more I used what I was given to supply definition and character to the house." Although the result is considerably less formal than his urban interiors, many of the solutions are drawn from the same pool of ideas and techniques. *Stucco lucido*, a clearly defined entryway, materials that are appropriate to their setting, objects that share a certain language in common: these are trademarks of Molyneux's work—on Park Avenue and on a ski slope alike.

LEFT: A second sitting area in the living room, with a primitive American weathervane over the kilim-upholstered sofa.

RIGHT: The living room, with the television concealed. The table behind the sofa is Spanish colonial; the carpet is from India.

The house's Southwest flavor continues in the master bedroom, where the materials—pine, kilim, and antler—are consistent with the rest of the interiors. Native American Kachina figures are grouped on the side table.

167

CHAPTER TEN

Trump Tower Aerie

The words "Trump Tower" usually conjure three things: extraordinary views; contemporary, if rather bloodless, architecture; and a touch of glitz. Certainly this apartment, when Juan Pablo Molyneux first visited it, could have been easily summarized by these qualities, but they were qualities which—except for the views—neither Juan Pablo nor his clients found particularly congenial. They had another goal in mind altogether: a European aerie that just happened to be floating in the Manhattan sky, fifty-seven floors above Fifth Avenue.

The former resident, a gallery owner, had rendered a suitably gallery-like interior: all-white walls, a ceiling lowered to accommodate spotlighting, a plain parquet floor. The rest of the finishes were standard-issue Trump Tower, which Molyneux describes as "pretty dismal," adding, "I think it's intentional, though. They seem to expect you to come in and do your own thing."

And so Molyneux did. He knew that his clients had chosen the apartment for the views, and he let these, together with the clients' art collection and their wish for a traditional home, cue his design for the interiors. The floor plan he liked and left intact, but he raised the ceilings and installed cove lighting, both of which helped amplify the box-like volumes of the living room and the gallery. Then he set about introducing a more classical vocabulary into the contemporary space. In the foyer he installed faux limestone walls and a black-and-white marble floor in the manner of the English Edwardian architect Edwin Lutyens. He continued the same floor into the ample adjoining gallery, but he paneled the walls here and in the living room in rich burnished koa. The living room received koa wainscoting and moldings to match; even the metal window surrounds were given a faux koa treatment, so that they would blend seamlessly into the walls.

Perhaps his most audacious choice for the living room was the eighteenth-century parquet de Versailles that was fitted into the twenty-foot by forty-foot space and gives it a most authentic, and unexpected, period flavor. It even creaks like the authentic parquet it is and only seems odd—or remarkable—when you look out the

Above: Detail of the dining table.

Left: The dining area brings together eighteenth-century Italian sphinxes and a suite of chairs by David Linley, which reinterpret the Swedish originals Molyneux used in his 1995 Kips Bay living room (see Chapter Twelve).

The gallery and hall share a Lutyens-inspired marble floor; the gallery's
rich koa paneling continues into the living room. Sculpture (left) is
Rodin's *Mighty Hand* and (right) his *Age d'Airain*. The photographs in the
gallery are by Stieglitz and Lewis Hine.

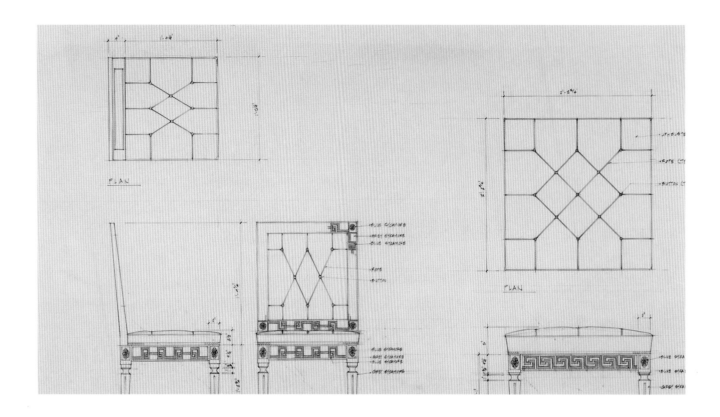

windows at the swirl of modern Manhattan. "The parquet is curious," Molyneux
concedes, "but isn't it curious to be sleeping on the fifty-seventh floor? I wanted my
clients to forget that they were on top of hundreds of other people. By using the
parquet, I was able to think of the apartment as being on the piano nobile of a
period building."

There is no avoiding the views, however, and of course Molyneux didn't want
to. He installed only minimal, fixed panels for curtains. Less obviously, in his choice of
furniture, textiles, and objects, he favored (by way of color) the greens and browns
of Central Park and (by way of line and scale) pieces of unusually vivid design that
would not be washed out by the views. In the living room, these include a pair of
nineteenth-century German Regency chairs with lion motifs, a pair of lamps made
out of bronze lions, a dining table whose base is a pair of eighteenth-century Italian
sphinxes, and an eighteenth-century painted English cupboard with bronze owls
applied to its doors. The designer claims that this bestiary was assembled purely by
happenstance, but one can't help feeling that these animals, powerful creatures all, were
chosen because of their capacity to hold their own against the insistent city skyline.

The owners' art collection, which includes several sculptures by Rodin,

Drawings by Picasso, Matisse, and Degas hang in the living room; the sculpture in the foreground is Rodin's *Vase des Titans*. The bronze owls on the eighteenth-century English cupboard are part of a varied bestiary that animates the apartment's furnishings. Rodin's *Burghers of Calais* stands on the cupboard; a canvas by Conrad Kramer hangs above.

drawings by Picasso and Degas, and canvases by Cy Twombly and Jim Dine, is distributed throughout the apartment and helps personalize the elegant polished interiors. Indeed, the interiors seem, in places, to have been created specifically for the art, particularly the muscular Rodins.

In the bedrooms, Molyneux modulated his palette, upholstering the master bedroom, for example, in a fabric that depicts a romantic Italian landscape. He added moldings, changed doors, and introduced onyx into the bathroom. Ever practical, he designed built-in bookshelves here, as he did in the guest room.

The apartment is not cowed by the city, nor does it try to compete with it: characteristically Molyneux, it makes a strong assured statement while remaining respectful of its setting. "It works well on a beautiful day, when you do nothing but gaze out the windows," observes the designer. "And it works on a wintry day too, when you're in a cloud and see nothing but white."

The living room, with its striking view over Central Park. The sculpture is Rodin's *Eve*.

CHAPTER ELEVEN

A Fifth Avenue Flat

T HERE ARE TIMES WHEN a New York apartment resembles an archaeological site: layers of decoration—some visible, some obscured—can encapsulate the bygone styles of the second half of the twentieth century just as vividly as the sedimentary ruins of an ancient civilization evoke a much more remote world—and worldview. The decision facing the designer, of course, is how many of these layers should be integrated into the apartment's newest incarnation and how many should be stripped away and replaced with a new vocabulary entirely.

In the case of this elegant prewar apartment opposite the Frick Collection on Fifth Avenue, Molyneux found strong traces of the building's original and mostly classical aesthetic: amply proportioned rooms, strong moldings, and a good parquet floor in the living room. At the same time, however, there was evidence—not all of it attractive—of various approaches taken in later decades. When the apartment was renovated in the early 1970s, for example, its gallery gained a marble floor that struck Molyneux as "extremely sixties and not all that easy to work with, although the client asked me to." Other additions from that period, discovered by Molyneux through old photographs, included black marble columns, red walls, and a living room open to the library, all fairly representative of 1960s taste. These, in turn, had been super-seded by a different treatment in the 1980s: wall-to-wall sisal carpeting, yellow striped wallpaper, glazed moldings, and abundant chintz. "It was a typical English country look," the designer explains. "And I don't think it made the best use of the interior architecture."

Molyneux, naturally, chose to take a more neoclassical approach. His clients sought an apartment that was "Continental and cosmopolitan," although they asked to keep new construction to a minimum. The designer's solutions, therefore, were mostly confined to reworking surfaces and making them as animated as possible.

Consider the gallery. Faced with the given of the gray-and-white marble floor, Molyneux treated the walls and moldings with two faux stone finishes that relate to the floor while also creating a strong presence of their own. Against this tailored

Molyneux chose to treat the first part of this apartment's gallery in his familiar neoclassical manner; the second half takes its cue from the living room and is upholstered in the same fabric. The console is nineteenth-century Italian and has dogs whimsically supporting the top.

The living room orients in two directions. At one end an eighteenth-century Coromandel screen has been separated into two pieces; the left-hand half conceals a television. The chandeliers are nineteenth-century Italian; the Aubusson rug is also nineteenth-century.

background he set furnishings that were in their own way quite architectural: an Italian directoire console whose sobriety is relieved by the dogs that support the top, a neoclassical mirror, Regency sconces, and Russian chairs. "These pieces keep up with the floor and the molding," Molyneux explains. "They have a similar power and mass."

In one of the apartment's earlier renovations, the gallery was rather arbitrarily divided in half by a plaster arch. Molyneux chose to treat the gallery's second half as a kind of antechamber to the living room. While the marble floor remains continuous, the walls change: instead of a stone finish, they are upholstered in a golden beige striped satin that continues into the living room.

Molyneux repeated this kind of visual leapfrogging in several places to help integrate the apartment's common rooms. The living room mantelpiece, for example, which replaced a reproduction pine mantle from the interior's English country period, is Italian directoire, and emphatically black. Its color and lines help connect the living room to the gallery, but they also manage to balance the room's most imaginative sleight-of-hand: one of the client's requests was that the living room orient equally to the fireplace and a large-screen television; Molyneux solved the problem of concealing the television by splitting an eighteenth-century Coromandel screen— also dark and emphatic—and hinging and motorizing one half. One screen, as it were, "screens" another.

Because the living room is focused in two directions, Molyneux decided to set a double sofa in the center. Symmetry becomes the room's leitmotif: chandeliers, trophy panels, Roman heads, and obelisks pair up in a conscious effort to keep the room balanced and interesting enough, not incidentally, to hold its own against the striking view of the Frick Collection across the street.

While the designer replaced many elements of the apartment's English country incarnation, others he had to retain and modify. In the library, for example, Molyneux "inherited," as he puts it, the pine paneling and cabinetry. His solution was to apply a darker wood stain and introduce Molyneux red in the carpet and textiles. In the dining room, he took a more radical approach: the floor had not weathered well (the sisal had been glued down directly on top of the existing wood), so he replaced it with a period parquet de Versailles. "This of course set the atmosphere instantly," observes the designer. He further erased the English country elements by changing another pine mantelpiece to a marble one, upholstering the walls in yellow and beige satin, and selecting furniture from periods that are increasingly associated with Molyneux's interiors: a Regency dining table, a set of Russian chairs,

The other end of the living room centers on the fireplace, whose surrounding wall Molyneux treated "as a kind of vignette—it's perfectly symmetrical, and it incorporates the beiges, golds, and blacks that dominate the room." Terra cotta figures on the tables are ancient Roman; the mirror is English Regency.

a French Empire jardiniere. Molyneux treated the window, which looked out on a postwar white brick building, with an elaborate curtaining. "The room had many doors and a bland view—a typical New York dining room in many ways—so I decided to make it very decorated," says Juan Pablo. "The interest is all on the surface."

As Molyneux's surfaces now join—or, actually, replace—the layers of time past, does the designer have any thoughts about how his approach will age? "One of the reasons you draw on a neoclassical vocabulary," he answers, "is that it has a long and appealing history. If you choose objects of beauty and quality and arrange them with confidence, you have an excellent chance of withstanding fashion. Truly good taste should be eternal, after all."

LEFT: The master bedroom, overview and detail. The armchairs are nineteenth-century Swedish; the writing table, by Emilio Terry, is from the 1930s; and the bench at the foot of the bed is English Regency.

RIGHT: The master bath, where a cut crystal owl hangs over the window.

Molyneux installed an eighteenth-century parquet de Versailles floor in the dining room and replaced its pine surround with an English marble mantelpiece. The table is Regency; the Russian chairs are upholstered in horsehair. Their medallions echo the medallions on the wall.

CHAPTER TWELVE

Molyneux at Kips Bay and at Large

Summarizing an interior designer's career is never easy, but it is a particular challenge in Molyneux's case, given his versatility, his restlessness, and his disinclination to be slotted into ready-made categories. A provocative road map to his work during the last decade does begin to crystalize, however, when two aspects of his craft are brought forward for closer scrutiny: Molyneux's smaller, less housebound projects, and the rooms he has created over the years to benefit the Kips Bay Boys and Girls Club.

From time to time during his career, Molyneux has left conventional interiors behind and set off in an idiosyncratic direction. Sometimes he has been prompted by a specific commission or request, sometimes by his own whims or interests. Consider, for example, the doghouse he designed for a charity benefit in 1992. His "client" was his dog, Max, a much beloved Scottish terrier. Max, his master maintains, had a "noble, Palladian personality" and required a suitably noble and Palladian house. Molyneux sized the structure to Max: it is about three feet square and has a portico in front with four Corinthian columns and a pediment complete with Max's coat of arms, a pair of crossed bones. The house is made entirely of plywood, except for the floor, which is real marble and laid in a classic black-and-white checkerboard. Why marble? "It's a summer house," says Molyneux. "Nothing's cooler than marble."

The doghouse may be as much an example of Molyneux at play as Molyneux at large, but even when playing, it seems, he adheres to vigorous architectural principles. Inside the single-room doghouse ("Kitchen and bathroom are downstairs," the designer remarks dryly), the walls were broken into three different trompe l'oeil treatments: a wainscoting in faux marble, a band of painted silk draperies, and a frieze of "ancient Roman" Scotties. The exterior was given a classic, trompe l'oeil limestone finish and a faux slate roof, which was in turn completed with a set of finials Molyneux commissioned from an English firm that produces mascots for cars. Made of resin and painted to look like old copper, they depict standing and seated Scotties.

LEFT: A detail of the 1991 Kips Bay living room, featuring a sumptuous carved and gilded Italian mirror, one of a pair. The lapis obelisks are mounted on rock crystal animals; the chair is eighteenth-century German.

ABOVE: A detail of the ceiling mural, by Anne Harris, which Molyneux later installed in his office.

Earlier, on a somewhat more sober note, Molyneux was asked to design another curiosity for charity in 1990: a rectangular box that was meant to fit into a bookshelf. He was supplied with the overall dimensions, one foot high by two feet wide by one foot deep, and given free reign from there. Molyneux chose one of his favorite rooms, an entrance hall, to which he gave a strongly architectural, and classical, treatment: a gilded beamed ceiling, marbleized columns with Ionic capitals, and dentil molding. As in the doghouse, the floor is real, although instead of marble, this time it is made of jasper and lapis. The hall is illuminated by tiny hidden lighting fixtures and is presided over by an Egyptian crocodile god, donated by Edward Merrin of Merrin Galleries.

Molyneux was not content with rendering a simple diorama. Halls, of course, lead from one room to another, and he decided to lead the observer's eye in several directions as well. The box requires some contemplation to absorb fully. Peering to the right, the viewer beholds a library; to the left, a straightforward flight of stairs; directly ahead, a confusing tangle of staircases reminiscent of, and inspired by, Piranesi's *Carceri d'Invenzione*. Only Molyneux hasn't imagined allegorical prisons, as Piranesi did, so much as different routes to heaven.

ABOVE AND RIGHT: "It would have been ridiculous to minimize this remarkable space," the designer says of his 1991 Kips Bay living room. Among the old master paintings are canvasses by Veronese, Titian, and Veneto. The commode (right) is one of five early nineteenth-century reproductions of a commode originally made for Versailles.

*A*DIFFERENT KIND OF COMMISSION, more of a request really, came from Tiffany, which has twice asked Molyneux to design table settings for the store in recent years. Molyneux's first approach, the simpler of the two, was to imagine a lunch table in an eighteenth-century French chateau. Hence the tapestry tablecloth, which hints at the flexible nature of the meal—it's a true movable feast, which was the custom in eighteenth-century houses, where there were no fixed dining rooms. You ate where you wanted to: a table was carried in, a tapestry flung over it, and people drew up chairs and sat down. Molyneux placed his table before another tapestry, which he hung as a curtain, and next to an English Adam serving table.

For his second Tiffany table setting, Molyneux created a complete environment. After finding four plastic Chinese-style columns in a store that makes theatrical props, he settled on a chinoiserie theme, using the columns to support a red silk pagoda. He borrowed a set of English Queen Anne red and gold lacquer chinoiserie chairs and arranged them around a table he fabricated from lapis and stone. The Tiffany china had its own chinoiserie theme. Molyneux's favorite red, naturally, predominated.

Red surfaces again in what is perhaps the most quixotic of Molyneux's assorted projects, the Harley-Davidson motorcycle he customized in 1995 with the help of Paul Sullivan at Ronnie's Cycle Sales in Pittsfield, Massachusetts, a dealership not far from his country house. Molyneux has been a longtime motorcycle rider, and it seems natural, perhaps even inevitable, that he would eventually be tempted to create a motorcycle of his own.

Two years earlier, Molyneux had arranged to have another model, a Dyna Glide, entirely chromed by his local dealer; every component ended up glistening, he explains, "like silver thunder." After noticing a brand new engine at Ronnie's one day, Molyneux learned that he could use it to create a motorcycle from scratch—or almost from scratch: he was not able to tinker with the frame and the engine, but most other components he could modify or piece together from a variety of sources. Molyneux elongated and curved the gas tank in order to allow it to nestle into the gentle bend of the frame; he pushed back and lowered the seat; he reshaped the rear fender, created a triangle-shaped unit to house the motorcycle's computer, and widened the rear wheel. Then he had the entire motorcycle painted a combination of red and desert taupe. While the Dyna Glide was entirely chromed, the Pro Street FXR—the Molyneux Harley—became a study in the designer's favorite, by now trademark, color: red.

A Tiffany table setting with a chinoiserie theme.

Molyneux's 1988 Kips Bay dining
room was already fitted with
handsome landscape panels, which
were painted during the 1920s
by Allyn Cox. They helped set the
tone for the lively room.

*R*EVIEWING THE FOUR ROOMS THAT MOLYNEUX DESIGNED FOR THE Kips Bay Boys and Girls Club decorator show houses between 1985 and 1995 is like taking a condensed tour of his work over the past decade, except that, instead of traveling from place to place, the observer travels through time and is given a chance to see the designer evolve in sped-up motion. Created at intervals of approximately three years, these rooms link the period between Molyneux's arrival in New York and the establishment of his thriving design practice.

The Kips Bay show houses have been a charitable tradition in New York since 1973; all proceeds from admission are donated to the Kips Bay Boys and Girls Club in the South Bronx, which runs an extensive after-school program in sports and the arts for youths between the ages of six and eighteen. Given free reign over a single room, the designer often displays his best or most versatile side in these fantasy interiors—"fantasy" because there is no client with whom the designer must collaborate and because he often borrows choice pieces of furniture, accessories, and paintings from willing antique dealers and art galleries. The interiors are temporary installations of the designer's craft; assembled for three weeks each spring, they are taken apart again at the end of the show, like a stage set or window display.

Temporary though they may be, the rooms are nonetheless exceedingly solid and real: the designer often restores the shell of the interior, and while he may borrow the components of the room, he is still responsible for the cost of painting, upholstering, mounting, and insuring the project.

Sometimes he takes his cue from the house's exterior architecture or an existing detail in the room—a molding, a fireplace, or a mural. Sometimes, however, he sets off in his own direction, as Molyneux did in 1985, the first year he participated in Kips Bay, when the room assigned to him was an undistinguished attic.

The show house in 1985 was a much-remodeled Beaux-Arts limestone town house on Manhattan's East 62nd Street, but an attic is an attic and Molyneux felt free to do with it what he liked. The design world of the mid-eighties was heavily influenced by postmodernism, with its heavy borrowings and samplings from different periods of architecture and interior design, and the palette at the moment was particularly subdued. Molyneux turned his back on this vogue and created a bright red room, which he envisioned as a gentleman's—maybe even a general's—library with a bar attached.

"It was a pastel house with a red poppy on the top floor," Molyneux explains. He imagined the room for himself (thus the red) and chose what he calls "masculine, rather severe, almost military" furniture and accessories. These included a Napoleonic daybed upholstered in stripes, a pair of Anglo-Afghan Regency armchairs, a Lucite head of Alexander the Great, and, on the coffee table, a cluster of reproduction Chinese warriors. Serpent prints and ancient Roman torsos of athletes or soldiers continued the tone of military campaign or conquest, which was echoed in the curtain fabric, whose camels and palm trees, Molyneux suggests, evoke a conquest of the Middle East.

In a somewhat different mood, the designer created a bar out of a small space adjacent to the attic. Enlisting the help of Lucretia Moroni (for the first time) and drawing his inspiration from the Café Florian in Venice, Molyneux installed painted chinoiserie mirrors and panels in the bar. Why chinoiserie? "My imaginary

A view of Molyneux's first Kips Bay room, from 1985. The torso is Greco-Roman, the English mirror nineteenth-century, and the daybed by Jacob. Molyneux red and neoclassical motifs are already in evidence.

general wanted to conquer China too," Molyneux says blithely. "No matter what," he adds, "there was nothing safe or careful about the room. It was fun and unexpected." Also unexpected was Molyneux's introduction to Paige Rense, the editor of *Architectural Digest*, who discovered his work here and soon after published one of his first completed projects in New York, his own town house on East 67th Street. Kips Bay launched Molyneux's relationship with Paige Rense, which has been a fundamental influence on his career. The editor has found patterns and directions in Molyneux's interiors that he hasn't always been entirely aware of, seeing, even before the designer did, that he was striving to break down the barrier between architecture and design. She has also resisted pigeonholing him as a one-note designer, choosing to show examples of Molyneux's work in the magazine that have ranged from the most classical of his projects to his Harley-Davidson motorcycles. "Her interest," he says, "has been vital and all-inspiring."

Three years later, in 1988, Molyneux returned to Kips Bay, moving down a few floors—but up in significance—to the dining room of a long narrow 1920 Georgian house on Park Avenue. Built during the twilight of private house construction on Park Avenue, the house is a subdued but elegant piece of Upper East Side domestic architecture, with a focal Palladian window, a peaked roof, and a facing of mellow brick. The dining room contained, in addition, a treasure: a series of chinoiserie landscape murals by Allyn Cox, which the owner rightfully insisted on keeping, as did Molyneux. He gladly had the silver- and gold-leafed murals restored and used them to guide his treatment of the rest of the interior.

Molyneux's work here is carefully calibrated to, and respectful of, the murals. For the curtains he found a silk fabric, first manufactured in the twenties, that had enough silver in it to relate to the silver in the murals. He designed a carpet in what he calls the "chinoiserie mood"—there's a hint of the 1920s here too—and found a pair of unusual Chinese lacquered armoires. Made during the early eighteenth century, they were originally hat cupboards in a Peking palace. The cupboards were so large that Molyneux had to remove the windows in order to bring them into the room.

The nineteenth-century porcelain zodiac figures (more blue, more Chinese) came from Molyneux's own house, but he departed in his choice of a set of late eighteenth-century Gothic revival dining room chairs. He liked them for their architectural quality and their burnished patina, which contrasted with, and helped ground, the painted and lacquered surfaces of the rest of the interior. As a final whimsical note, Molyneux took great pleasure in writing out the name cards. "People are usually so pretentious in these show houses," he explains. "They invite the Lord of This to dinner and the Princess of That. My guests were John, Mary, Susan, and Howard."

The bar, also from 1985, was modeled on the Café Florian in Venice. Lucretia Moroni painted the mirrors.

Certainly the grandest of Juan Pablo's Kips Bay rooms was the living room he designed in 1991. The house that year was a 1912 brownstone on East 70th Street that had a particularly handsome double-height living room. The rest of the house had been diminished during previous restorations, but this room retained its ornate, carved wooden paneling. Although contemporary to the house, it was done in the eighteenth-century style.

The paneling was oppressively dark, and Molyneux began by stripping and waxing it, which imbued it with a gentle, golden hue and lightened the room considerably. The ceiling remained white, although he complicated it by installing a Michelangelo-inspired mural to its central panel. Commissioned from Anne Harris, it depicts the trumpets of doom dressed up in Scalamandré fabric. "I wanted all the guests to be up on the ceiling," Molyneux says, "since the room had everything else in it but people."

"Everything else" is a fairly understated summary of a collection of extraordinary paintings and furniture. In planning the room, Molyneux believed that it would be ridiculous to consider it anything but grand, and he decided to go all out. "I thought of the room as a cocktail party made out of very chic furniture and paintings," he says. "I invited a variety of people and wouldn't take no as a response."

Accepting Molyneux's "invitation" in 1991 were (on canvas) Veronese, Titian, Veneto, and Rauschenberg. Why Rauschenberg? Because Molyneux believes that objects of first-rate quality go together no matter what their period and because he is consciously *not* designing historical reproductions and likes to introduce a contemporary note as a reminder. Also in attendance were Angelica Kauffman, the noted Swiss-English painter of eighteenth-century furniture—she is responsible for the pair of commodes that flank the fireplace. She was joined by the anonymous but nevertheless gifted craftsmen who produced a pair of eighteenth-century, gilded Italian mirrors, Aubusson tapestry panels and rugs, and an ancient Roman portrait bust.

For the 1995 Kips Bay show house, Molyneux was assigned the living room of a 1905 town house on the Upper East Side. Designed by the then popular mansion architect C. P. H. Gilbert in the French Renaissance style, the house was in excellent repair. Once again, Molyneux was able to take a cue from an existing detail, in this case the room's baroque plaster moldings and wall panels.

Baroque, to Molyneux as to most people, means intense and ornate, and his first impulse was to pare the room down. He did this by removing a few of the more overwrought garlands, taking away a built-in mirror over the fireplace, and painting the walls a gray-green celadon and the ceiling a washed steel blue. Molyneux then complicated the space again by introducing one of his rigorously geometric painted marquetry floors instead of the more obvious choice of an Aubusson or Oriental rug. The floor's design was inspired by Russian marquetry Molyneux had seen and admired at the Pavlovsk Palace in St. Petersburg. Typical of Molyneux, however, was his decision not to pay excessive attention to the striking floor once it was installed. "I furnished the room independently," he explains. "It was as if we moved into a house that already had the floor, and we ignored it."

Nevertheless, Molyneux's nod to Russia continued in his use of an eighteenth-century Russian desk, which is as strong as the floor, if not quite as dominant in the room. From here, Molyneux jumped countries and selected a suite of eighteenth-century Swedish chairs and stools. With their original characteristic cool gray paint, they provided a link to the pale elegant walls and ceiling, but with their severe lines and Greek key carvings, they still managed to hold their own against the darker and

The diorama Molyneux designed
for a charity benefit (12 in. high,
12 in. deep, 24 in. long). The room
he chose to depict is a neoclassical
entry hall, with a floor rendered
in lapis and jasper.

A preparatory drawing and a
realized portion of the painted
marquetry floor Molyneux added
to his 1995 Kips Bay living room.

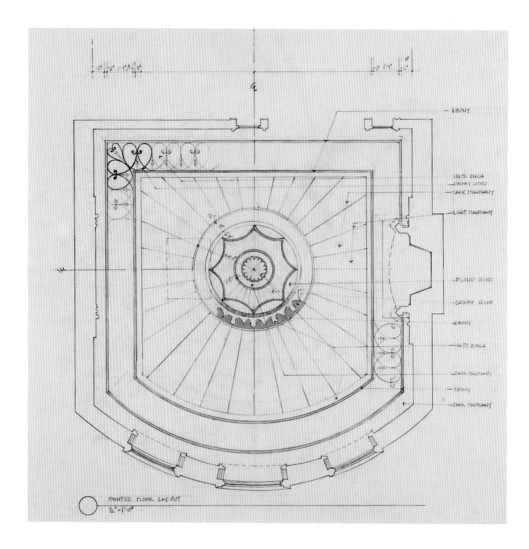

more substantial Russian furniture. To keep up with all this strong wooden furniture, Molyneux felt he needed to use vivid fabrics for his upholstery and turned to the Paris firm of Braxton for his silks and pressed velvets.

Finally, Molyneux commissioned a series of *animalerie* panels from Anne Harris. "You have to be careful in your use of paintings when you have a room with built-in panels like this one," Molyneux observes. By creating pictures specifically for the interior, he was able to fit them exactly, both in size and sensibility. They have a feeling of playfulness that leavens and somehow integrates the many sensibilities present in the decor.

Although there are several different periods and elements represented in Molyneux's 1995 Kips Bay room, the designer maintains that they share a common language. "Instead of words," he explains, "furniture is being used to make conversation. And I like to think that this conversation is cultivated enough to range among a variety of topics."

The confident quality of this conversation is characteristic of much of

Molyneux's recent work, which has become versatile enough to cross cultures and periods with considerable ease and flair. Juan Pablo has evolved substantially from that first room in his parents' apartment, with its burlap curtains and *Seven Samurai* poster glued to the ceiling. His craft, grounded early on in the different disciplines of modernism and neoclassicism, has been deepened and cross-fertilized by his travels, his reading, and, of course, the experience of producing many dozens of rooms.

Behind each Molyneux interior there is usually a memory of the interiors that preceded it, as well as an anticipation of those to come. Molyneux himself expects that in the next ten years, he will build on his earliest foundations. He sees his interiors becoming at once more historically accurate in the architecture and design components they incorporate and at the same time freer and open to still more elements of fantasy. The interplay between the real and the imagined first captivated the designer when he was starting out. It has animated and enlivened his work for twenty-five years now and—it seems inevitable—will continue to do so in the future.

The furniture in Molyneux's 1995
Kips Bay living room moves in
paradoxical directions: the painted
Swedish chairs and stools relate to
the gray-green walls, while the
darker Czech commodes and desk
connect more strongly to the faux
marquetry floor.

ABOVE: A detail of the 1995 Kips Bay living room, featuring an *animalerie* panel by Anne Harris and eighteenth-century Italian sconces.

RIGHT: The eighteenth-century Swedish chairs, which David Linley reinterpreted for the Trump Tower apartment (see Chapter Ten). The urns are Swedish and made of *porphyry*; the tea set is *porcelaine de Paris*.

FOLLOWING PAGE: The motorcycle in a vibrant—what else?—Molyneux red.